LEAD WITH A
COACHING
MINDSET

LEAD WITH A COACHING MINDSET

How the Best Leaders Unlock Potential

DAMIÁN GOLDVARG

BK

Berrett–Koehler Publishers, Inc.

Copyright © 2025 by Damián Goldvarg

All rights reserved. No portion of this work may be reproduced or transmitted in any form or by any means, electronic or mechanical, including photocopying and recording, or by any information storage or retrieval system, or be used in training generative artificial intelligence (AI) technologies or developing machine-learning language models without permission, except in the case of brief quotations embodied in critical reviews and certain other noncommercial uses permitted by copyright law. For permission requests, please contact the Copyright Clearance Center at marketplace.copyright.com/rs-ui-web/mp.

Berrett-Koehler Publishers, Inc.
1333 Broadway, Suite P100
Oakland, CA 94612-1921
Tel: (510) 817-2277
Fax: (510) 817-2278
bkconnection.com

ORDERING INFORMATION
Quantity sales. Special discounts are available on quantity purchases by corporations, associations, and others. For details, please go to bkconnection.com to see our bulk discounts or contact bookorders@bkpub.com for more information.
Individual sales. Berrett-Koehler publications are available through most bookstores. They can also be ordered directly from Berrett-Koehler: Tel: (800) 929-2929; Fax: (802) 864-7626; bkconnection.com.
Orders for college textbook / course adoption use. Please contact Berrett-Koehler: Tel: (800) 929-2929; Fax: (802) 864-7626.

Distributed to the US trade and internationally by Penguin Random House Publisher Services.

The authorized representative in the EU for product safety and compliance is
EU Compliance Partner, Pärnu mnt. 139b-14, 11317 Tallinn, Estonia,
www.eucompliancepartner.com, +372 5368 65 02.

Berrett-Koehler and the BK logo are registered trademarks of Berrett-Koehler Publishers, Inc.

Printed in the United States of America

Berrett-Koehler books are printed on long-lasting acid-free paper. When it is available, we choose paper that has been manufactured by environmentally responsible processes. These may include using trees grown in sustainable forests, incorporating recycled paper, minimizing chlorine in bleaching, or recycling the energy produced at the paper mill.

Library of Congress Cataloging-in-Publication Data

Names: Goldvarg, Damian author
Title: Lead with a coaching mindset : how the best leaders unlock potential / Damian Goldvarg.
Description: First edition. | Oakland, CA : Berrett-Koehler Publishers, Inc, [2025] | Includes
    bibliographical references and index.
Identifiers: LCCN 2025003639 (print) | LCCN 2025003640 (ebook) | ISBN 9798890570727 paperback
    | ISBN 9798890570734 pdf | ISBN 9798890570741 epub
Subjects: LCSH: Leadership | Executive coaching
Classification: LCC HD57.7 .G66397 2025 (print) | LCC HD57.7 (ebook) | DDC 658.4/092—
    dc23/eng/20250505
LC record available at https://lccn.loc.gov/2025003639
LC ebook record available at https://lccn.loc.gov/2025003640

First Edition
33 32 31 30 29 28 27 26 25   10 9 8 7 6 5 4 3 2 1

Book production: PeopleSpeak
Cover design: Ashley Ingram

To the leaders who dedicate themselves to shaping a healthier, brighter, and more compassionate world.

To my parents, coaches, and clients—your inspiration has guided me to unlock my potential and become the best leader I can be.

CONTENTS

FOREWORD

When I coach leaders who want to improve the impact of their communications with peers as well as their team members, I never start by asking about their behavior. I start with saying, "In your position today, define what you think is the purpose of leadership." They often respond with words similar to "get results" or "motivate people to give their best." Then I ask, "When you see yourself getting results or motivating action, what are you doing when at your best?" Even today, they describe their directive behavior of telling, sharing, or guiding. Rarely do they describe what they did to enable people to think and act on their own.

Before I found coaching, I worked as a training manager in three corporations. In my classes, employees always said they wanted their leaders to listen more and ask questions to better understand what their challenges and desires were, and they wanted to be treated with respect for what they knew. They wanted the behaviors and regard from their leaders but said they didn't expect it.

Over the last twenty years, the desire for genuine leadership engagement and trust evolved to being an expectation. The gap between what leaders think they should be doing and what employees want from them continues to widen.

In *Lead with a Coaching Mindset*, Damián Goldvarg captures this phenomenon in a profound way by exploring how the global pandemic amplified the rift. His exploration of what leaders are called to do in our post-pandemic world is accurate and thorough and provides a map to guide the often-difficult transformation leaders must make.

Starting with developing a coaching mindset, this book offers a comprehensive manual for leaders to use their presence to create the safety and trust needed so individuals and teams willingly engage in the mentally creative process of coaching. Then, Damián gives some essential tools, including to listen for the meaning behind pivotal words and expressions, how to courageously and respectfully challenge old thinking and limiting beliefs, and how to adeptly use silence. As a result, leaders become thinking partners in their conversations where insights emerge, possible solutions are discovered, and the confidence to embrace change grows.

Leaders don't have to become professional coaches to proficiently use a coaching approach to initiate these powerful conversations. When leaders use reflective statements and questions that prompt an inward exploration, people hear their words, see how their beliefs form their perceptions, and explore the root of the emotions they are expressing. Without being told to change their thinking and behavior, they then see the gaps in their logic, the assumptions they imagine about the future with no evidence, and the fears that are keeping them from moving forward.

Daniel Kahneman, in his classic book, *Thinking, Fast and Slow*, said we provide value when we provoke critical thinking in others because our brains block us from thoroughly analyzing what we think about situations when left on our own to sort out our thoughts. The brain prefers holding on to past beliefs over accepting new ideas and unpredictable outcomes. Yet when someone else reflects our thoughts and asks about meaning and options, we can see "outside the boxes of our thinking" to consider new ideas. When using the coaching skills in this book, leaders develop the ability to perform the vital function of overriding protective brains to stimulate exploration and innovation.

Giving employees and peers a judgment-free, safe space to observe their thinking is critical to both business and personal growth. Damián blends well the development of both coaching presence and essential skills. People leave their conversations with leaders feeling seen, heard, and valued in addition to owning the many insights and creative solutions that came to light.

Lead with a Coaching Mindset is a gift as well as a guide for the post-pandemic leader. I am honored to be a part of sharing this work with leaders around the world.

Marcia Reynolds, PsyD, author of *Breakthrough Coaching*

PREFACE

We cannot become what we want to be by
remaining what we are.

—MAX DE PREE

You have likely read many books on leadership. And if you are a manager, you probably read many books on management. But this book is different. The soul of this book is simple and unique: to be a better leader in an environment that is volatile and uncertain, be a better coach.

The framework of this book is based on the eight core competencies of the International Coaching Federation (ICF). This global organization accredits professional coaching programs and certifies coaches, setting ethical and professional standards to advance the professional practice of coaching.

My professional commitment to the development of leaders globally spans over thirty years. From that initial moment to the present, as I sat down to write the book you have in your hands, a tremendous number of individuals who have successfully navigated the corporate world, academia, and nongovernmental organizations have placed their trust in my leadership development services. They sought to establish more satisfying relationships with their colleagues and their loved ones while staying aligned with their company's vision and maximizing their personal potential.

Although I have authored or coauthored ten books on coaching, this is the first one in which I directly address leaders with whom I collaborate, offering my coaching services and effective leadership training. I focus on the competencies they need to maximize their performance, develop their team members, and enhance their emotional, social, and cultural intelligence.

I take pride in following my calling to foster the professional and personal improvement of leaders who, each in their own way, work toward meaningfully contributing to building a better, more humane, peaceful, and harmonious world.

HOW THE BEST LEADERS UNLOCK POTENTIAL

I absolutely believe that people, unless coached,
never reach their maximum capabilities.

—Bob Nardelli

What are the new paradigms and skills that leaders need to navigate the volatile, uncertain, complex, and ambiguous world? How do effective leaders respond to the multiple economic, political, social, technological, environmental, and emotional challenges of the times we are living in? How can we collaborate in creating learning opportunities and healthy workspaces by applying coaching skills? In this book, we will explore these questions.

This book was born as I uncovered the mindset and philosophy in my work as a leadership coach. Many of the skills and abilities I am hired to help leaders develop are similar to those I had learned to develop as a professional coach myself.

Professional coaching is not directive. It seeks to put the client first—coaches seek to partner with another human being to spark their own path of discovery and self-accountability. An effective coach does not give advice, impose goals, or tell the client what to think or do. The effective coach is a thought and accountability partner and mirror and is not "in charge." To some, this type of service may seem the opposite of leadership.

The word *leadership* is believed to originate from the Old English *laedere*, meaning "the one who guides or brings forth" or "directing a ship or animal." The inference is that the leader provides the moving force and motivation. However, my experience as a coach has taught me that the type of partnership today's coaches provide is exactly the type of support contemporary leaders need to be effective!

In this book, I aim to define what it means to be a leader with a coaching mindset and the benefits it brings to organizations, preparing them to navigate present and future challenges. To achieve this, I will draw on an adaptation of the ICF's model of eight competencies for professional coaches, my personal experience, and interviews with global leaders.

I have learned that leaders often make the greatest progress when they develop the same skills we seek to develop in professional coaches. My goal is for leaders to find tools in these pages that allow them to reflect on their work and incorporate new skills suitable for propelling them to the best version of themselves, within a context that increasingly promotes higher levels of partnership and collaboration and requires sophistication in understanding and supporting the emotional states of their team members.

This global landscape serves as a reminder that when leaders develop coaching skills, they create healthy organizational cultures that foster well-being and satisfaction. They also, in a way, invite shared creativity and become magnets for talent. The most valuable individuals within organizations—the high performers—seek to work with these leaders precisely because they know they won't be working for them but alongside them.

I hope that each chapter of this book, which I intend to use as a reference in the leadership development training programs I offer, helps you clearly understand what is specifically expected of a leader capable of producing extraordinary results in our increasingly complex times. I will share examples, challenges, and strategies to navigate these times and provide opportunities for reflection and planning.

LEADING AND COACHING
WHAT NEEDS TO CHANGE

The leader with a coaching mindset does not seek to dazzle with their own light but helps others to ignite theirs.

—Damián Goldvarg

I write these pages after years of global and social upheaval caused by disruptions in the economy, environment, government, and—most notably—public health. Few would dispute we live in a "new normal" that requires innovative approaches.

According to psychologist Diego Quindimil, a "psychologist leader" is needed, someone who provides empathetic motivation and promotes mental health at work.[1] This leader should demonstrate closeness and support, putting hierarchies aside to achieve the greatest possible person-to-person connection. This can be quite challenging but is crucial for organizations where employees are considered the most valuable resource.

TODAY'S LEADERSHIP CHALLENGES

When faced with ambitious and challenging goals, people may experience high levels of stress. In my work in leadership development for over thirty years, I have observed that corporate messages often express that employee well-being is a top priority. Nonetheless, many times leaders' behaviors and expectations around performance are not aligned with these messages. Managers may be sending mixed messages by highlighting the importance of well-being and at the same time providing multiple tasks to be implemented in a short time. This work pressure is not unique to companies but is also present in nonprofit, governmental, and educational organizations.

What do we expect from these "new normal" leaders? They need to be more emotionally and socially intelligent, more supportive, and less authoritative. They need to develop higher levels of sensitivity to work with people from different cultures and provide higher levels of autonomy.

While organizations have been investing in leadership development through coaching for years, more people are realizing that hiring external coaches is not enough. Leaders need to develop coaching skills to take responsibility for the development of their direct reports rather than delegating this task solely to professional coaches.

Additionally, leaders who neglect investing in their coaching skills and do not pay attention to team development may not only fail to attract talent but also risk falling behind with outdated management strategies, especially if they insist on using hierarchy as a ramrod of influence.

Recently, I was hired by a leader to coach her on developing her coaching skills. Lorena shared that she interviewed a project manager to work on her team. She was impressed with the candidate's credentials, experience, demeanor, and emotional intelligence demonstrated during the interview process. When my client finally offered the job, she was surprised to learn the candidate declined the offer. When my client asked why the candidate decided to work at a different company, she was told she had not positioned herself as a coach or someone invested in developing her staff. My client was shocked. She decided she had to develop her own coaching skills since that was a blind spot for her.

What does this suggest to you? Does this mean more employees and job seekers are assuming that a coaching environment is becoming common? Does it indicate some managers are not changing with the times and are thus surprised by new expectations?

I am far from the first to see the connection between coaching and leading. For example, in their book *It's the Manager: Moving from Boss to Coach*, Jim Clifton and Jim Harter write that bosses need to become coaches, and coaching must set expectations, be offered continuously, and create accountability for employee success.[2] New generations at work seek partners, not bosses. They desire clarity in expectations, purposes, assigned responsibilities, and regular feedback. A Gallup study reveals that employees engage in their jobs when in the following situations:

- They have bosses who involve them in the development of their annual goals. In such cases, they are four times more engaged than when bosses do not involve them.
- They have bosses who provide strengths-focused feedback weekly instead of once a year.

- Performance evaluation is linked to their professional development.[3]

In this study, Gallup's largest global research study regarding employees' experience, the focus was on how employees feel when considering their life and work so as to predict resilience and organizational performance. The researchers concluded the following:

- Six out of ten employees have "quietly quit," meaning they stopped engaging fully. They completed their work but didn't go beyond what is necessary, likely due to feeling disconnected and stressed.
- Only 22 percent of employees felt engaged at work.
- The low level of participation and engagement costs the global economy $8.8 trillion.
- A total of 44 percent of the respondents felt stress in their jobs the day before and 51 percent were actively seeking new employment.

When asked "What would you change to make work a better place?" 41 percent responded with culture, meaning how work is done. They value recognition, autonomy, growth opportunities, respect, and the opportunity to receive coaching. Only 28 percent indicated they would appreciate higher pay and benefits, demonstrating that the latter is not the most crucial factor for employees.

One of the most interesting results of the research showed that stress reduction is linked to the level of enthusiasm and work engagement. While the possibility to choose where to work is essential for stress reduction, the organizational culture that either promotes or hinders individual engagement is correlated with stress reduction. This finding is significant because leaders, by creating healthy organizational cultures, can promote this involvement.

The Gallup study suggests that developing coaching-minded leaders is crucial for team success and employee retention. A leader who provides coaching inspires engagement and retains employees who feel valued. This goal is particularly relevant now, when increasing the level of commitment, involvement, and participation has become more crucial.

DEFINITION OF COACHING

It is important to differentiate coaching and leading. A leader with a coaching mindset differs from a professional coach who has been formally trained and obtained credentials to support clients to maximize their potential.

The word *coach*, which has been used in a business context for over thirty years, was borrowed from the world of sports but originally comes from a Hungarian word meaning *carriage*. The word *coach* is also used for the economy section of trains and airplanes. It is also the word used in the United Kingdom for *bus*.

This association is simple: a coach accompanies a person on their journey from one place to another. This is supported by the International Coaching Federation (ICF), which defines the activity as "partnering with clients in a thought-provoking and creative process that inspires them to maximize their personal and professional potential."[4]

In this definition, two words require special attention. The word *partnering* is important because it emphasizes the act of cocreating the conversation as opposed to being the expert and providing direction and consultation. The philosophy of the ICF is that the coach-client relationship needs to remain a collaborative process to the greatest extent possible. This symmetry is crucial in the present era, with its increasingly remote-work environments. Collaboration is key, given the nature of the challenges and assuming an authoritative stance can be an obstacle to team engagement and loyalty.

Professional coaches inspire their clients and view them as whole beings with resources to find their own solutions rather than needing to be fixed. The clients are experts in their lives, and the coach provides a safe space for reflection and designs new ways of being and doing, leading them to become a new observer of reality with new possibilities of action.

Another key word in the definition is *potential*, as the focus is on developing what is latent to create higher levels of awareness, possibilities for action, and results that would not be achieved without that new awareness, learning, and support.

According to a study conducted in 2020 by the ICF and PricewaterhouseCoopers (PwC), coaching is one of the fastest-growing professional practices.[5] Researchers declared coaching to be one of the activities that experienced the most significant growth worldwide in 2019, generating approximately $2.85 billion in revenue.

The ICF and PwC study shows that the growth of the activity is related to not only the number of certified professional coaches but also to more leaders and managers adopting coaching practices.

Coaching is considered a suitable means for adaptation and positive change in organizations as it includes valuable tools for crisis management, optimizing emotional intelligence, and leadership development.

COMPETENCIES OF THE LEADER WITH A COACHING MINDSET

Leaders that demonstrate coaching skills are committed to the development of their team members. Such leaders understand the importance of their staff's personal and professional growth and invest time and resources to help them achieve it. The leaders' results depend on how well those under their supervision meet their objectives. They use coaching as a means to reach goals and as a methodology to inspire and motivate their team members.

Coaching leaders invest time in deeply understanding their staff, personally and professionally. Such leaders inquire into the staff's unique needs, challenges, and expectations regarding the social, economic, health, and political reality of the context in which they find themselves. Additionally, such leaders engage in conversations focused on developing the skills of their staff and colleagues, both for their current effectiveness and readiness for future jobs and events involving new challenges. They also dedicate energy to identifying strengths and weaknesses in their direct reports, allowing them to create plans to leverage strengths and address areas with improvement opportunities.

Khalil Dirani and colleagues in 2020 researched the leadership competencies and the role of human resource development in times of crisis, a response to the COVID-19 pandemic.[6] They found out that essential leadership competencies in such times include supporting individuals and organizations in overcoming limitations and fears. This support needs to translate into offering and demonstrating flexibility, communicating frequently, acting with transparency, showing empathy, reinforcing positive feedback, acknowledging the difficulties being faced, and sharing appreciation for work.

A case study that fits the description of a leader demonstrating key competencies during a crisis is Jacinda Ardern, the former prime minister of New Zealand, and her leadership during the COVID-19 pandemic.[7] Here's a breakdown of how her leadership aligns with the competencies described.

CASE STUDY: JACINDA ARDERN'S LEADERSHIP DURING THE COVID-19 PANDEMIC

New Zealand Prime Minister Jacinda Ardern was faced with the critical task of leading the country through the COVID pandemic, protecting public health, and minimizing economic impact. Here's how her unique approach saved lives.

1. *Go hard early*—Ardern focused on protecting the health and well-being of the population by quickly implementing strict lockdown measures. Her "go hard, go early" strategy emphasized the importance of swift action to mitigate the virus's spread. She acknowledged the psychological strain on citizens and promoted mental health

resources, encouraging people to seek help if needed. She also took these steps:

- She regularly adjusted policies based on the evolving situation and scientific data.
- She ensured the government's response plan was dynamic, shifting from a strict lockdown to a phased reopening based on real-time infection rates.
- She held daily press conferences and communicated directly with the public through various platforms, including social media.
- She built trust with her approach, as people felt they were getting honest and up-to-date information.
- She frequently acknowledged the hardships faced by citizens. She showed genuine concern for families separated by lockdowns, businesses struggling to survive, and essential workers risking their safety.
- She shared messages of solidarity, stressing the importance of working together as a "team of five million" to combat the crisis.
- She celebrated the efforts of frontline workers, healthcare professionals, and the general public for their resilience and commitment during lockdowns.
- She praised New Zealand's collective efforts, boosting morale and reinforcing the importance of shared responsibility in overcoming the crisis.

2. *Acknowledge difficulties and show appreciation*—Ardern openly discussed the economic hardships, the toll on

mental health, and the disruptions to daily life. Her appreciation extended to thanking citizens for following guidelines and making sacrifices to protect the vulnerable, which helped maintain public cooperation.

Under Ardern's leadership, New Zealand initially managed to control the spread of COVID-19 effectively, becoming one of the few countries to achieve periods of zero community transmission. Her response was widely praised for its decisive action, clear communication, and empathetic approach. Though challenges persisted with subsequent waves, her early actions helped reduce the overall impact of the pandemic on public health and the economy.

Her ability to connect with the public on a human level, combined with data-driven decision-making, played a significant role in New Zealand's initial success in managing the crisis.

This case study highlights how a leader can support individuals and organizations in overcoming limitations and fears during times of uncertainty by fostering a sense of community and resilience.

AWARENESS DURING A CRISIS

In times of crisis, leaders must have a full awareness of the situation, both for themselves and their direct reports and other colleagues. Particularly, they need to be aware of the stress and anxiety levels experienced by the team. Therefore, leaders need to remain visible and accessible, maintain calm, and, more than ever, model behaviors in the organization that prioritize the emotional stability of each person.

Leaders need to acknowledge the fear that impacts people, assign clear roles and purposes, and focus on learning and the emotions of everyone involved. Marcel Schwantes, a business writer and coach, emphasizes the particular value of being flexible, paying attention to responses that reveal emotions to work on, staying fully involved by actively participating, and listening to the opinions of employees.[8]

Among the most common challenges faced in crisis situations are uncertainty, the absence of reliable information, and unclear and changing objectives. People respond differently under pressure in critical times. Some accept change, while others resist it either openly or subtly. The need to deal with the complexity of situations and the ability to adapt to new realities require emotional support.

Dana Brownlee is a project management expert who has extensively considered the psychological skills effective leaders need to guide today's teams.[9] She argues that leaders in the post-pandemic era need to demonstrate these seven competencies:

- Candor and unambiguous honesty
- Consistent, reliable, and fact-based communication
- Empathy, born out of understanding the emotional challenges of grief and anxiety
- Management of hybrid teams
- Flexibility and adaptability
- Humility, including knowing how to ask for help
- Active listening

Note that Brownlee bypasses some historical skills, such as creating metrics, setting agreed goals, and measuring performance.

Fernando Perla, technology manager at Banco Santander, says, "The leaders with a coaching mindset understand that everyone has their potential, and not everyone is developable in every aspect. They focus on developing the potential of the individuals on their team, maximizing their talent, [and] prioritizing the impact they can have on organizational results and the clearly defined actions required to produce results."

When leaders receive coaching training, they are better prepared to develop their team members.

THE CRISIS AT GLOBEX

During the COVID-19 pandemic, Globex International was hit hard.[10] It had to deal with remote working, lockdowns, employees facing severe family compromises, and considerable stress. The firm's international supply chain was taking a hit. Management had to support its strained staff as much as possible to keep the business moving. Flexible work arrangements were clearly needed, which meant top management had to make sure all managers recognized reality and would not fall back on the old definitions of the workplace. Employee burnout was not an option.

Constant communication with employees—every one of them—was absolute. Managers had to lead with empathy and, what's more, show it. Managers had to share their own stories of vulnerability, to enhance management's credibility. Everyone was vulnerable, and the potential loss of key employees had to be kept uppermost in mind.

The results showed that employees were not just surviving. They were overwhelmingly positive about the support and understanding management showed. Such a sentiment went a long way for employee retention and recruitment. Leading with a coaching mindset includes showing your own concerns and anxieties to be credible and trusted.

Who benefits when a leader effectively demonstrates coaching skills?

The leader—Leaders become a magnet for talent. Those seeking personal and professional growth choose to work with leaders who invest time and effort in developing their team members. They are aware that they will receive learning and growth opportunities, making the work more appealing. The coaching-minded leader understands that the results achieved by the people under their charge directly influence corporate outcomes and enjoys the satisfaction of seeing team members grow and reach new positions within the organization. If their teams grow, opportunities for the leader's own growth also expand.

The team member—Team members feel heard and valued, discover growth opportunities, and are prepared for future challenges. They, in turn, become inspired and generate a higher level of loyalty and commitment.

The team—A profound sense of shared responsibility and belonging emerges among the team.

The organization—Organizations achieve greater commitment and results from their employees. According to the ICF study mentioned before, companies that invest in coaching cultures attain superior economic results and engagement.

When a leader takes on the role of providing coaching, it fosters collaboration, loyalty, creativity, and the development of new ideas.[11]

DEFINITION OF LEADERSHIP

Just as I've defined coaching, it is important to define what leadership is. Leadership means the ability to lead, and to lead, we need to inspire and influence.

Warren Bennis believed that "Leadership is the capacity to translate vision into reality."[12] John Maxwell stated, "Leadership is influence—nothing more, nothing less."[13] Similarly, Tim Stevenson suggested, "You are a leader if you know where you are going and are able to persuade others to go along with you."[14] All these definitions align with the idea of the leader designing a desired future and inspiring people to build it.

But leadership in organizations needs to be based on principles and values, aiming toward goals that are honorable and good for all. No selfish hidden agendas. We will discuss this in chapter 2 on ethics. We also believe that leadership needs to be based on honest communication and not manipulation or deception.

Research about exceptional leaders found that they of course are all unique, but what they have in common is that they know themselves.[15] They have intentionally identified their strengths and areas for more opportunity, and they work on them.

Leadership scholars such as Daniel Goleman, known for his work on emotional intelligence, emphasize the importance of self-awareness for effective leadership.[16] Additionally, leadership models such as transformational leadership, servant leadership, and authentic leadership all highlight the significance of self-awareness as a foundational trait for successful leadership.

The latest research on leadership focuses on several emerging trends that are shaping the field:[17]

Agile leadership—Agile principles are increasingly important, emphasizing flexibility, adaptability, empowerment, collaboration, and a strong customer-centric focus. Leaders are encouraged to develop these traits to effectively respond to rapid market changes and foster innovation within their teams.

Personalized leadership development—A trend is growing toward personalizing leadership development programs to better align with individual leaders' unique needs and career aspirations. This approach includes individual assessments, tailored learning plans, and personalized coaching, aiming to enhance engagement and effectiveness.

Skill expansion and continuous learning—As artificial intelligence (AI) continues to influence the workplace, leadership skills must evolve. Leaders are expected to continuously expand their skills, embracing AI and fostering a culture of continuous learning and adaptation within their organizations.

Ethical use of AI—With the increasing deployment of AI in various business functions, leaders need to address the ethical implications and maintain trust by being transparent and responsible in how AI technologies are implemented and used.

Hybrid work and flexibility—The transition to more hybrid work environments requires leaders to balance the needs for in-person collaboration with the benefits of remote work. Flexibility in work arrangements is becoming crucial for employee retention and engagement. Not everyone is returning to the office, and scientists are nervous about other pandemics popping up around the world.

Diversity, equity, and inclusion (DEI)—People are supporting the integration of DEI into all aspects of leadership and organizational practices. Effective leaders are expected to actively support and implement DEI initiatives to foster an inclusive workplace culture.

These trends highlight the complex and dynamic nature of leadership development, focusing on both personal adaptability and the ethical use of technology, all within the context of changing workplace dynamics.

SIX LEADERSHIP STYLES

Daniel Goleman considers that organizational climate is influenced by leadership style, specifically by how managers motivate their direct reports, make decisions, and handle changes and crises.[18] The author identifies six leadership styles, explaining that all are required in different situations. As you learn about each style, consider which one you may use more frequently:

- Coercive style
  - Involves giving orders
  - Works well in crisis situations or with employees facing difficulties
  - May limit motivation
  - Is considered outdated and resisted by new generations

- Authoritative style (with authority, not authoritarian)
  - States objectives but allows space to choose how to achieve them
  - Better adapted to current demands than the coercive style
  - In times of uncertainty, employees require clear guidelines to develop their creativity in the workplace

- Pacesetting or innovative style
  - Sets the pace with high objectives
  - May lead to resentment with excessive demands
  - Post-COVID, new virtual work strategies and a changed relationship between workers and their job and connections with all parties, including clients, colleagues, and superiors, require the leader to be innovative and sensitive to the needs of their collaborators

- Affiliative style
  - Focuses on relationships, creates harmony, and boosts morale
  - Does not correct errors that lead to underperformance
  - Appropriate for the post-pandemic era but risks neglecting processes and results if energy is solely invested in relationships

- Democratic style
    - Involves everyone in almost all decisions
    - Very flexible and relies on individual responsibility
    - May create confusion
    - Still appropriate in the current era but requires the development of new skills to navigate situations where individual responsibility is absent

- Coaching style
    - Focuses on developing collaborators
    - Works well with employees who recognize their own opportunities for improvement and are willing to work on them
    - Less effective when there is resistance to change
    - Note: This is the style proposed in this book because it is considered key to the effectiveness of leaders in this era

While each of the styles is required in different circumstances, I believe that leaders often miss opportunities to apply the coaching style. Leaders need to be able to adapt their style to different situations and consider each of the six styles to apply them at the appropriate moment. The global study conducted in 2020 by the ICF in collaboration with PricewaterhouseCoopers determined that leaders are increasingly training in coaching skills to enhance their effectiveness and create the highest levels of productivity, satisfaction, and loyalty.

APPLYING THE ICF MODEL TO BRING COACHING AND LEADING TOGETHER

Research on organizational cultures conducted by the ICF in 2014 found that organizations with a strong coaching culture work with internal and external coaches and train their managers to acquire coaching skills.[19] According to the study, these organizations receive a higher degree of engagement from their employees, translating into superior economic results compared to competitors that do not foster this type of culture.

Promoting the development of coaching skills in managers often results in significant gains for the organization, with a multiplier effect, as trained employees develop their colleagues much more effectively.

In this book, we will adapt the ICF framework, which guides the activity of professional coaches and includes eight competencies, to the work of the coaching-minded leader:

- Foundation (the two competencies related to ways of being)
  - Demonstrates ethical practice
  - Embodies a coaching mindset

- Cocreating the relationship
  - Establishes and maintains agreements
  - Cultivates trust and safety
  - Maintains presence

- Communicating effectively
  - Listens actively
  - Evokes awareness

- Cultivating learning and growth
  - Facilitates client growth

The ICF prefers not to use the term *leader coach* and chooses to refer to the "leader applying coaching competencies" to distinguish them from the professional coach. In this book, we will use the words *colleagues, direct reports,* and *team members* when we refer to the person working with the leader during coaching conversations.

MOVING ON

The importance of leaders developing coaching skills is identified by abundant research, as this chapter outlines. But what about what motivates a leader, including a leader with a coaching mindset? We have all seen managers or leaders who make the right calls regardless of personal issues, motivations, and incentives. But what about the other kind of leader? The kind whose agenda gets in the way of a basic foundation of recognizing right versus wrong?

CHAPTER SUMMARY

The current times pose multiple challenges, requiring leaders to demonstrate resilience and adaptability. It's an era of different work environments that are not likely to return to the old days of offices up and down the aisle.

A psychologist leader provides empathetic motivation, promotes mental health at work, and fosters closeness and support, transcending hierarchies for maximum person-to-person connection.

The ICF framework emphasizes that coaching inspires clients to maximize their potential, viewing them as whole beings with the resources to find their own solutions, creating new possibilities by becoming new observers of reality.

Coaching-minded leaders are managers dedicated to the professional growth of their team, investing time and resources to do so.

The distinction between coaching-minded leaders and mentors lies in the latter providing information and direction, while the former invites their team to find their own answers and solutions.

Being a coaching-minded leader has four main benefits: (1) the leader becomes a talent magnet, (2) the team members find growth opportunities, (3) the team experiences a deep sense of shared responsibility, and (4) the organization gains increased commitment and results.

Promoting managerial development in coaching skills yields significant gains for organizations, fostering a coaching culture with a multiplying effect.

Leaders need to demonstrate flexibility, empathy, and transparent communication; reinforce feedback; recognize work; and acknowledge challenges. That includes recognizing fear in times of crisis, assigning clear roles and purposes, and focusing on learning, energy, and emotions. It includes emotion-revealing responses, engagement, and active listening.

Here are the seven key competencies for today's leaders: (1) candor and unambiguous honesty, (2) consistent, reliable, and fact-based communication, (3) empathy, (4) management of hybrid teams, (5) flexibility and adaptability, (6) humility, and (7) active listening.

The Goleman six leadership styles are coercive, authoritative, pacesetting, affiliative, democratic, and coaching.

The trend is increasing among leaders to receive training in coaching skills, aiming to enhance effectiveness, productivity, satisfaction, and loyalty in their teams.

ETHICAL LEADERSHIP
AND COACHING
THE ENGINE OF MATURITY

Ethics is nothing more than the rational attempt to
figure out how to live better.

—FERNANDO SAVATER

Ethics are fundamental for the performance of a coaching-minded leader. In our experience, we found that one of the main qualities followers seek in their leaders is their trustworthiness. A leader who displays a strong sense of ethics will almost always inspire trust. And trust is the foundation for coaching. Without trust, coaching is not possible.

Therefore, in this chapter, I will focus on defining what ethical leadership is and developing its principles. The aim is to encourage a leadership practice guided by ethics, emphasizing personal integrity, respect for the identity of team members, and ethical maturity. Furthermore, through the exploration of ethical dilemmas, I will prompt you to reflect on the expected behavior of a leader striving to coach team members and influence the course of their organization.

WHAT IS ETHICAL LEADERSHIP?

Ethical leadership includes respect for the beliefs, values, dignity, and rights of others. A coaching leader demonstrates ethical leadership when behaving with integrity and committing to the well-being of others, showing respect, and celebrating both similarities and differences.

First, though, we need to distinguish ethics from morality. Morality refers to a set of norms and principles based on the culture and customs of a particular social group. In contrast, ethics (or leadership ethics at least) are people's individual behavioral code that allows them to discern personally between right and wrong.

An easy way to remember the difference is to note that morality applies to a group, such as customs to be obeyed for proper behavior, while ethics stem from an individual's reflection on which actions are desirable and which are not. All physicians have the universal morality to "First, do no harm." However, physicians can reflect this morality differently in their own personal ethics.

It is impossible to understate the importance of the leader's ethics to the organization at large. In fact, "good enough" can never describe a leader's ethics. Ethical leadership actually requires adhering to *higher* standards than employees have and becoming a role model. Leaders' behaviors influence organizational culture as they set guidelines, develop vision, and share their values and actions to shape employees' behavior.

The ethical behavior of the leader may indeed influence and determine the morality of the organization.

THE SCENE: MANIPULATING DATA

A coaching client discovered that her team had manipulated data to make a project look more successful than it actually was. The pressure to meet targets can lead to unethical behavior, sometimes called "cooking the books."

In previous sessions during the coaching process, we explored the importance of engaging the team in decision-making and identified how many times the team may have had better answers than my client did. When my client discovered that the project was behind, she was not sure what to do. She decided to consult with the team. My client expressed the importance of integrity as one of her key values and also reasserted this value as one in alignment with the organization.

After the discussion, instead of covering up the mistake, the team decided to report the issue to upper management and propose a plan to rectify it. Upper management appreciated the team's transparency, and the team learned the value of ethical practices. It corrected the data and faced the challenges together, leading to stronger teamwork and integrity.

Researchers Linda Treviño, Laura Hartman, and Michael Brown argue that to become an ethical manager, one must first be an ethical person, attentive to their level of integrity, uprightness, and honesty outside the workplace.[1] It simply is not possible to "play act" ethics during work hours and abandon them outside of work. Regarding the managerial aspect, these authors emphasize that an ethical leader strives to influence others to behave ethically by transmitting norms and values and being an example while also ensuring compliance with what is transmitted.

The experts identify three measures taken by effective ethical managers:

- They are visible models of ethical behavior.
- They regularly and persuasively communicate ethical standards, principles, and values.
- They use the rewards system consistently.

Coaching leaders align with the moral code of the organization to which they belong, specifying expected behaviors and those deemed inappropriate according to organizational values. For instance, some organizations prioritize collaboration as a fundamental value, expecting employees to strive for teamwork to achieve established goals.

Usually, ethical guidelines are included in the employee handbook, which, it's worth noting, is often overlooked, and employees may not have read it. Sometimes, there is inconsistency between what is written, what is said, and the behaviors of leaders. In the words of Google's Camilo Gómez, "Whenever possible, I try to demonstrate. Modeling is powerful. Much more powerful than saying."

LEADING WITH INTEGRITY

David, a coaching client, shared that one of his team members had made a wrong business decision and was working hard to cover it. He found out randomly about this decision and was not sure how to manage the situation and confront his direct report to make it a learning experience versus firing him. He brought the situation to our coaching session and we discussed blind spots for him as well as for his direct report. We explored what kind of leader he wanted to be and how to coach this person to use this decision as a learning opportunity. We also explored different scenarios.

David decided to invite his team member to a meeting and gave him an opportunity to be honest and vulnerable and admit his mistake. It worked out. They discussed integrity and the importance of acknowledging mistakes versus hiding them, and David emphasized the importance of keeping him informed and showing integrity.

PRINCIPLES OF ETHICAL LEADERSHIP

It is easy to slip into generalities and complexity when discussing ethics. One set of rules cannot be applied to every situation and every person. However, what does ethics actually look like in action, and how can we be more specific?

Peter Northouse's lifelong reflections on ethical leadership are foundational.[2] He shares the following five principles of ethical leadership:

- *Respect others*—Treat others as human beings with needs and never as a means to an end. Respect involves listening with genuine attention to employees, being empathetic, and showing an interest in different opinions.

- *Serve others*—Be altruistic, prioritizing the well-being of employees in plans. Ethical leaders pay attention to the interests of others and act in a way that benefits everyone.
- *Be just*—Care about fairness and justice in decisions, treating all employees the same way. Treat others differently only when their particular situation demands it, with clear and reasonable motives based on moral values.
- *Be honest*—Don't just tell the truth but also be open and disclose information as fully and completely as possible. Honesty requires vulnerability to share beliefs that demonstrate authenticity, even if it means showing imperfections.
- *Create community*—Pay attention to personal and others' goals, caring about the common good. Strive to create bonds that increase a sense of belonging.

PRACTICES OF ETHICAL COACHING

Let's move from principles to the four key practices that ethical coaches—and coaching leaders—need to demonstrate according to the ICF:[3]

- Having personal integrity
- Showing respect for the identity of collaborators
- Being mindful of language
- Maintaining confidentiality

Having Personal Integrity

Ethical leaders model what they expect from direct reports and colleagues with their own behavior. The word *integrity* is used to describe the quality of being consistent, unified, and whole. To inspire and create coaching cultures, leaders need to cultivate consistency between what they say and do and be as transparent as possible. Honoring and fulfilling promises and commitments are critical behaviors. Additionally, it is essential to tell the truth and always be sincere, even when information cannot be shared due to confidentiality. It is important to explain this to team members.

Ethical leaders are committed to ensuring that their behaviors align with the personal and organizational values they have internalized. Consistency between being, saying, and doing is fundamental.

Ana Escalante is one of the first ICF Master Coaches in Mexico and has led a powerful career working with executives and coaches. She has written a book on the topic of integrity and suggests four key ingredients that apply to leaders and professional coaches alike:[4]

> *Self-awareness*—These leaders know their own preferences, likes, values, and qualities that distinguish people. They understand everyone's dreams and the legacy everyone wants to leave in the organization.

> *Self-legitimization*—Leaders granting themselves validity. The word *legitimate* comes from the Latin *legitimus*, meaning "fixed by law." It signifies declaring a person skilled or fit for something. Self-legitimization involves giving oneself the right to be authentic, accepting both virtues and flaws, and allowing oneself to make mistakes, learn, and dare to be genuine.

> *Self-completion*—Living a complete life means living without unfinished business. It involves knowing that agreements and

promises made to oneself are fulfilled and meeting commitments to others. These leaders feel inner peace when what they say and do are in total alignment.

Self-love—Leaders can observe themselves with respect and without fear, acknowledging limitations, judgments, and mistakes. They develop healthy self-esteem and self-worth and identify their own needs.

Escalante asserts that coaching-minded leaders recognize when the behaviors of their employees, colleagues, or clients do not align with ethical guidelines and take appropriate actions to change those situations. They pay attention to others when they exhibit behaviors that are not aligned with the values of the organization or are unethical to gain profits or results. They also notice if others have a short-sighted vision that prioritizes the self over the collective, short-term gain over long-term vision, or the privilege of some at the expense of others.

An example of a conflict of interest is when a candidate for employment has an internal advocate in a higher leadership position in the organization. This situation is not unusual, especially as employers have incentive rewards for employee referrals. But in this case, outright pressure comes from a superior in another department who is a relative or friend of the candidate. The ethical stance here is to report and seek help from human resources to tone down the pressure.

Showing Respect for the Identity of Team Members

Ethical leaders—ones with a coaching mindset—commit to understanding the people they work with, recognizing them as unique human beings with specific needs, rather than as objects oriented toward producing results. In this sense, they are sensitive to their experiences, values, and beliefs, fostering satisfying relationships and healthy organizational cultures.

Leaders with a coaching mindset understand the need to acknowledge and appreciate the differences in age, gender, race, religion, sexual orientation, and skill level among their direct reports and colleagues. To achieve this, they develop sensitivities related to emotional and cultural intelligence, including using appropriate language that demonstrates an understanding of the subtleties that can cause discomfort and resentment among colleagues. They may be curious about the preferred pronouns of employees: he/him, she/her, they/them.

Martin Denzel, previously a researcher at Altos Labs, shares these words of wisdom: "The leader culturally does not treat everyone in the same way but rather in a way specifically tailored to a person's needs and identity."

Being Mindful of Language

The language we use reflects our beliefs, expectations, needs, and concerns. Language is like water to a fish—it remains invisible until it is no longer there. Our language is invisible until we pay attention and realize how we create our reality with it.

The words we use not only describe reality but also create it. When we declare that we are going to do something, a new reality becomes possible. For example, before writing this book, I had to declare that I would do it, and after sharing my intention with colleagues, I began the task. Every time we say yes or no, new possibilities for our lives open or close.

Paying attention to language also allows us to recognize cultural context and identify the need to ensure that our language is clear, precise, and respectful and does not offend people from different cultures. This requires awareness of the language we use to prevent misunderstandings and intentionality in choosing the words we use. Alexis Ekizian, Google's head of midmarket sales in Buenos Aires, shared this example:

> In multicultural teams, it is important, when speaking, to focus on inclusion. We have had debates about how important it is to be mindful of what one says, even without bad intentions. For example, in Argentina, when something is challenging, it is common to say, "This is a Chinese thing." This is a small example of how someone can be unintentionally offended, in this case, someone of Chinese nationality. If something like this happens, it is important to talk to the person and provide necessary explanations, and then discuss with the team the importance of what is said. Putting oneself in each person's shoes is part of building leadership.

Maintaining Confidentiality

Discretion builds trust. However, in the workplace, some information cannot be kept confidential. Examples of this include bullying, sexual harassment, and substance abuse at work. Leaders are expected to keep personal information that their collaborators shared with them in confidence, to the extent possible, meaning as long as it does not compromise the integrity of the organization. Ethical leaders know how to maintain confidentiality of the information both shared with them by their team members and that was entrusted to them by their superiors.

Leaders who improperly share personal information about other colleagues compromise their credibility. The colleague may wonder, "If my boss shared information that was not appropriate about a peer, how can I be sure they won't share my personal information with other colleagues?"

When working for an international leadership development company, I had a colleague I trusted, and I shared some personal information that she inappropriately shared with our boss. When I learned about it, I confronted my colleague, who apologized. I know we are human and we make mistakes, but even though I forgave her, I never felt I could trust her completely with personal information. Trust may be regained but will never be the same.

This can happen in any organization. People have lunch together. They inquire about someone's bad mood at the coffee station. But leaders need to be role models and be careful about sharing information that is not for them to share.

ETHICAL MATURITY

Developing ethical maturity gives leaders a compass to make challenging decisions. Ethical maturity is the ability to make decisions based on ethical standards while considering various perspectives and conditions, such as information, experience, analytical ability, intuition, empathy, and compassion.

Michael Carroll and Elisabeth Shaw are counseling psychologists and consultants in organizations, and they defined ethical maturity as "The reflective, rational, emotional, and intuitive ability to decide actions that are right or wrong or good or better and having the courage to implement them, being responsible for the decision, able to live with it, and integrating learning for future actions."[5]

Ethical maturity involves the ability to reflect on and examine various aspects of the situation deeply, working rationally, logically, and emotionally. These authors argue that it develops over a lifetime and is a process that goes from decision-making based on a dogma that does not allow analysis (for example, decisions based on religion or values learned at home) to an openness to consider multiple perspectives and possibilities, taking into account the context, people, and relationships.

Carroll and Shaw identified six components of ethical maturity:

- *Creating ethical sensitivity and mindfulness*—Awareness of oneself and the impact of our behaviors on others is the first step toward ethical maturity. This includes the ability to be aware of our values and motivations; how we use power in relationships; our physical, emotional, mental, and spiritual self-care; and the development of compassion and empathy.
- *Conscious ethical discernment and decision-making*—This is the ability to reflect on and make ethical decisions. Mature ethical decision-making requires flexibility; consideration of both rational and emotional or intuitive elements, information, and experience; and the willingness to take risks or play it safe.

- *Implementing ethical decisions*—This consists of analyzing supporting elements and obstacles to implement decisions. Making a decision is not enough when dealing with ethical challenges. There may be a gap between making and implementing a decision. The latter requires courage, commitment, and resilience. There may be obstacles to implementing the ethical decision: conflicting values, personal and professional consistency, competing commitments, and collusive stances.
- *Ethical accountability and moral defense*—This is the ability to publicly defend our decisions and connect them to our principles. It requires us to articulate in language why we did what we did.
- *Ethical sustainability and peace*—This is the ability to live with the decision made and be at peace with oneself, learning from the process and letting go of concerns.
- *Learning from the experience and integrating new learning into moral character*—This consists of using the learning from the experience to enhance self-awareness and become more ethically competent.

ETHICAL DILEMMAS

Coaching leaders often encounter ethical dilemmas in their daily routine—unexpected situations that make them question the most appropriate decision. In these moments, it's important to assess which information to pay attention to for making the best possible decision. As seen in the previous section, the development of ethical maturity involves using not only reason but also intuition and emotions.

Ethical dilemmas arise daily, and mature leaders know not to rush to judgment. For example, if they realize that a colleague is being untruthful, they have to decide whether to stay silent or communicate what they know. A valuable tool is the brief examination provided by the Ethics Centre, a nonprofit organization based in Australia, which suggests asking these six questions before making a decision:[6]

- Would I be happy if this decision appeared in tomorrow's news?
- Is there any universal rule that applies in this case?
- Will the proposed action make the world a better place for everyone?
- What if everyone did this?
- What effect will this action have on my reputation or the reputation of my organization?
- Is the proposed action consistent with my values and principles?

Effective leaders often face dilemmas that have no ideal solution. In such situations, they need to make tough decisions that involve sacrificing good things for others that are better.

A PERSONAL STORY

Let me share a personal experience. I was invited to work for a brewer to provide workshops in high schools on the effects of alcoholism and alcohol abuse in people's lives. When I was interviewed, I was asked how comfortable I felt working for a brewer.

I drink beer and thought I would be providing a valuable service to the community by increasing awareness of alcoholism and contributing to preventing alcohol abuse. I started facilitating the workshops, but something did not feel right. Even though I was providing useful information, my salary was coming from companies that profit by selling the alcohol causing the many deaths from drunk driving.

In the past, I had easily decided not to work for the tobacco industry. I had family members who died from smoking. But alcohol was not as clear. Even though I decided to take the job, a few months later, I quit. Something was not aligned with my values. That was not as clear at the beginning. And this realization is very common. Many times, the boundaries of what is acceptable are not as clear. Working with my own coach helped me clarify how this job was not aligned with my personal values and why it was important for me to quit.

Most ethical dilemmas are not clear-cut. Exploring them and getting support is key to overcoming the challenges. What becomes counterproductive is self-deception. Sooner or later, we will have to face how our decisions are not aligned with our values and how important it is to take appropriate action.

MOVING ON

By now, you are wondering how you will get to this ideal of the manager as a good coach. It takes some work. It requires recognizing cultural differences. You need to be able to stop and reflect on situations. Intuition is important, but intuition based on objectivity and not preconceived prejudices is key. You need to develop and master your inner coach and recognize when you may need to reach out for confirmation or objectivity. It's all about your coaching mindset.

CHAPTER SUMMARY

Ethics are crucial for the performance of a coaching-minded leader.

A coaching-minded leader demonstrates ethics by behaving with integrity and committing to caring for others, showing respect, and celebrating both similarities and differences.

Ethics is different from morality. Morality refers to the set of norms and principles based on the culture and customs of a particular social group. Ethics is the personal decision-making process as a result of understanding and applying morality and allowing an individual to discern between right and wrong.

Ethical leadership is a process in which people are influenced to achieve goals in a socially responsible manner.

Ethical leadership requires leaders to adhere to higher standards than their employees and become role models.

To become an ethical manager, one must first be an ethical person, maintaining integrity, uprightness, and honesty outside the workplace. Effective ethical managers are visible models of ethical behavior; regularly and persuasively communicate ethical standards, principles, and values; and use the rewards system consistently.

The five principles of ethical leadership are (1) respecting others, (2) serving others, (3) being just, (4) being honest, and (5) creating community.

Coaching-minded leadership requires behaviors comparable to those of a professional coach: having personal integrity, showing respect for the identity of team members, using language carefully, and maintaining confidentiality.

Ethical leaders are committed to understanding the individuals they work with, recognizing them as unique human beings with specific needs, not as objects aimed at producing results. They understand the importance of recognizing and appreciating differences such as age, gender, and race, among others, and they develop emotional and cultural intelligence for this purpose.

Leaders need to be mindful of their language, ensuring it is clear, precise, and respectful and does not offend individuals from different cultures.

An ethical leader maintains confidentiality of information shared by both subordinates and superiors.

Ethical maturity is like a compass. It helps direct one's path between the rational and the emotional, the analytical and one's intuition, the logic of a situation and how one reflects on it.

Six components of ethical maturity have been identified:

- Creating ethical sensitivity and mindfulness
- Conscious ethical discernment and decision-making
- Implementing ethical decisions
- Ethical accountability and moral defenses
- Ethical sustainability and peace
- Learning from the experience and integrating new learning into moral character

MINDSET IS EVERYTHING
DEVELOPING YOUR
INNER COACH

Every now and then a man's mind is stretched by
a new idea or sensation, and never shrinks back to
its former dimensions.

—OLIVER WENDELL HOLMES SR.

Leaders who develop a coaching mindset value their team members not only as employees but also as human beings with needs, goals, and dreams. The term *mindset* is used to describe an attitude or inclination. Leaders' attitudes are foundational to the success of their working relationships.

Embodying a coaching mindset also means engaging with colleagues from a place of appreciation for their development and growth. It involves consistently investing time in personal and professional development for both leaders and their direct reports, providing resources for acquiring new skills and seeking opportunities for applying what has been learned. Leaders need to continually work to be appreciative partners, not just superiors and subordinates.

FIVE KEY CONCEPTS OF A COACHING MINDSET

In this chapter, you will learn what it means to embody a coaching mindset, explore its associated behaviors, and read examples. There are five key concepts related to this mindset according to the ICF framework:

- Trusting employees as responsible individuals with the capacity to make appropriate decisions
- Committing to continuous development
- Creating spaces for reflection
- Being aware of context and culture
- Using one's sense of self and intuition for the benefit of the team

Francesco Bassoli, vice president of global procurement at Alcoa, says,

Having a coaching mindset entails helping people find a common direction, develop competencies, and achieve their goals. It involves assisting them in defining where they are and where they believe they need to go—their journey. For me, defining that journey and supporting them is acting as a coaching-minded leader. This includes identifying gaps, finding ways to fill those gaps, ensuring there is a common understanding, and determining the competencies needed to navigate the path effectively.

Next, I will delve more deeply into these elements of the coaching mindset competency, following the guidelines of the ICF.[1]

Trusting Employees as Responsible Individuals

Coaching leaders trust that their team members have the necessary capacity to make decisions that positively impact results, and when that's not the case, they take responsibility for the consequences. Viewing their team members as resourceful and with multiple capabilities involves relating as adults and trusting that decisions will be made judiciously.

What happens when the leader disagrees with a decision made by a team member? The key is to determine whether the decision could negatively affect the business or other individuals. In such cases, and contrary to coaching practices, the leader may need to intervene to take control or ideally, if the situation allows, create a new moment of reflection, a coaching space that enables learning and a new shift in perspective before taking action.

Leaders applying coaching competencies are responsible for obtaining results. This is not the case when hiring external professional coaches. Leaders with a coaching mindset will need to make decisions at opportune moments that may not align with their team members' preferences or negatively affect some of them. Additionally, they may need to wear the hats of a mentor, teacher, or guide when appropriate.

Alexis Ekizian, head of midmarket sales at Google SpLatam in Buenos Aires, Argentina, points out, "Coaching is ingrained in Google's culture. Almost all managers have this mindset, with very few exceptions to this unwritten rule. They might not be aware that they are providing coaching, and they may lack a theoretical framework, structure, or methodology. However, they are, for example, providing coaching to me since I joined the organization."

Committing to Continuous Development

To maintain the curiosity that comes with professional growth, leaders embodying a coaching mindset are open and flexible and continue learning. Typically, leaders who invest time and effort in developing their team also invest in their own growth. They work with a coach, participate in training, read books, and seek opportunities to evolve every day.

Here are some continuous learning resources to help with development:

Newspapers—Stay informed about global, national, and local happenings, as effective decisions require this information. I like the Wall Street Journal for its focus on global issues and for its section on the Future of Everything.

Harvard Business Review—This highly prestigious and widely consulted source for continuous leadership learning offers monthly publications, books, and articles on leadership.

TED Talks—These engaging presentations are under twenty minutes long and inform and inspire. They are impactful and easily accessible video recordings.

YouTube channels—Explore a wide range of channels, including ours. We have over 450 videos at youtube.com /DamianGoldvarg.

Podcasts—Numerous options are available in the market based on personal preferences and professional goals.

Industry-specific magazines and publications—Stay up to date with resources relevant to your industry.

AI platforms—Generative artificial intelligence applications such as ChatGPT provide helpful learning resources.

The mere act of reading this book reflects your commitment to continuous development. Some leaders express a desire for more time for their personal development, but their behaviors don't align with this wish. While they acknowledge the importance of continuous learning, they don't take the time for it. Aligning values and priorities is important, as discussed in the previous chapter.

This challenge presents a coaching opportunity for leaders who struggle to prioritize professional development, not just in planning but also in implementation. What will it take for them to find the time and commitment to invest in their own continuous development? Could it be that these leaders are focused only on the present and not on acquiring the skills needed to face future challenges?

Creating Spaces for Reflection

I have been focusing on creating spaces for reflection in recent years, particularly in the continuous development of profes-sional coaches and supervisors. I addressed this in a book titled

Coaching Supervision, published in 2017, where I underscored the importance of continuous reflection in a space of cocreation and dialogue.[2]

The word *reflection* comes from the late Latin *reflexio* and describes the action of going back. When we reflect, we go back to make sense of and find new interpretations for our experiences. Reflection involves exploring our beliefs, emotions, and behaviors to learn from them and achieve a higher level of effectiveness. Consequently, I consider it essential to create spaces for reflection, setting up time for conversations to examine, interpret, or make sense of the work we do with our colleagues.

Leaders may find spaces for reflection, both with their own superiors and with their direct reports, to create an environment that allows stepping back from specific issues and envisioning new possibilities for being and doing in that context.

I believe that leaders would benefit from working with a professional coach who has the skills to inspire, challenge, and collaborate to create a reflective space, exploring blind spots, ethical dilemmas, and emotional reactions, among other things.

Nancy Kline, in *More Time to Think*, pointed out that an increase in the capacity for reflection is related to the relevant context and how people are treated.[3] Kline explained that specific behaviors of the listener determine the quality of thoughts. The listeners' behaviors influence the reflective space to such an extent that this listening is more critical than the intelligence, education, and experience of the ones doing the thinking. In other words, attentive listening generates the opportunity to reflect for others.

Creating an environment conducive to reflection is linked to a way of being in the world rather than a series of techniques.

Leaders seeking effectiveness need to question whether they are genuinely interested in understanding what their direct reports are thinking and how they can create conditions of respect and support for creative thinking.

Kline presented ten elements that need to be taken into account to create creative spaces for reflection:

Attention—Genuine curiosity while listening fosters better thinking than when engaging with someone who interrupts or shows disinterest.

Equality—Treating those who are reflecting together as equals, disregarding hierarchical relationships, enhances better thinking.

Calm—Reflecting is more effective in a relaxed space rather than under pressure from urgencies and stressors.

Appreciation—Thinking is more effective when people are appreciated rather than criticized. Recognition needs to be sincere, specific, and concise.

Encouragement—Encouraging individuals to take risks and go beyond their usual ways of thinking leads to more effective outcomes. This requires creating a space full of trust, acceptance, and support.

Information—Using all available information promotes better thinking. Discarding information can be a hurdle to creative reflection, and the supervisors need to be attentive to detect if their thinkers are not sharing something, for example, because they dismiss it.

Place—Investing in resources, creating a suitable space for reflection, and demonstrating genuine interest in the participants leads to increased engagement.

Incisive questions—Asking exploratory questions that challenge assumptions achieves a better level of reflection, especially when exploring limiting beliefs. Challenging assumptions enables productive questioning and opens new possibilities for thinking, feeling, and decision-making.

Diversity—Appreciating differences in identity and ideas enhances thinking more than conveying the message that our thinking is better than others'.

Feelings—Expressing feelings, such as anger or sadness, leads to a better level of reflection than hiding or numbing them. Expressing common fears (of failure, humiliation, or exclusion, for example) allows for more creative spaces. Fear, conscious or unconscious, is a major obstacle to creative thinking. Unfortunately, it is also a taboo topic that often remains unexpressed and hinders the reflection process.

Being Aware of Context and Culture

When we talk about context and culture, we are not only referring to cities and countries. Diversity is much broader. It can be in terms of gender, sexual orientation, age, religion, and ability, among other factors. Sometimes, this diversity can create blind spots—perspectives we can't even see and therefore cannot explore. As mentioned earlier, the ability to work interculturally is also an ethical requirement for a coaching leader.

A systemic perspective is crucial to avoid these blind spots. Therefore, leaders with a coaching mindset need to be aware of the systems they are involved in, constantly being curious about what is happening in their economic, social, and political context. Leaders want to be aware of how circumstances around their teams may be affecting their performance.

In one of the organizations where I train leaders, one staff member committed suicide, which affected the team very much. People were grieving and needed an outlet to share their experiences. That space was offered by the leader and gave team members an opportunity to share their feelings and normalize their experiences. Effective leaders invite their colleagues to share their experiences and emotions instead of behaving like nothing has happened.

Using One's Sense of Self and Intuition for the Benefit of the Team

The ability to know oneself makes a significant difference in how we relate to the world. The distinction known as "self as instrument" means that leaders with a coaching mindset are aware and acknowledge that what happens to them and their ideas, body sensations, experiences, emotions, and intuitions can be a valid source of information for making personal and professional decisions.

Our experiences, such as our emotions or physical reactions, can provide useful information in the coaching conversation. If we bring ourselves into the equation, become truly present, and establish ourselves in the here and now, we can work efficiently to help team members develop awareness and realize what is happening around them. This will also require that we fine-tune our perception of what resides in our thoughts and our hearts, aligning all of that and incorporating it into the conversation.

CULTIVATION OF THE INNER COACH

The inner coach is the voice in our head that guides us to coach others and sometimes ourselves. This voice needs to be intentionally cultivated. We strengthen this voice by working with good role models, such as colleagues, managers, and professional coaches who support us in developing our decision-making criteria and challenge our behaviors to accomplish our goals.

Personally, I began developing an inner coach when I was very young. I believed everything was possible with hard work. When I was sixteen years old, I learned I could finish high school one year earlier if I studied by myself. When I shared my goal with my parents, they weren't supportive. They did not see any need for me to make such an effort. But I did not like high school and decided to do it even without their support. My inner coach helped me develop good study habits, discipline, and confidence in myself. I was able to take the exams and pass all the tests and finish high school a year earlier. I learned from that experience and became a licensed psychologist in Argentina when I was twenty-one years old. This inner coach has helped me accomplish many goals in my life, and the secrets included discipline, hard work, commitment, confidence, and the ability to ask for help.

Pam McLean, the author of the book *Self as Coach, Self as Leader* and the president of the Hudson Institute of Coaching, suggests that cultivating the inner coach is necessary for effective coaching.[4] She highlights six elements that need to be considered to develop this inner voice: presence, empathy, emotions and feelings, boundaries and systems, courage, and embodiment.

- *Presence* involves mindfulness practices that connect us with our experiences to enrich the way we relate, work, and coach. It includes paying attention to what is happening, noticing it, and being curious about it as well as noticing our body, heart, pulse, thoughts, biases, judgments, and desires.
- *Empathy* is the ability to feel and understand the emotions, circumstances, intentions, thoughts, and needs of others. With this, we can offer support and communicate sensitively, perceptively, and appropriately.
- *Emotions* are physiological responses that provide information about the world, and *feelings* are the conscious responses to these emotions. Naming the feeling allows us to take action. This process from emotion to action requires mindfulness. Recognizing, naming, and acting consciously enable leaders with a coaching mindset to manage their emotions effectively.
- *Boundaries and systems* refer to the tendency to develop flexible rather than rigid boundaries, allowing for an optimal level of separation. Boundaries can lead to disconnection if too rigid or demand our involvement in a situation and lead to overprotection if too open. Ideally, leaders listen while maintaining the appropriate distance. When Pam McLean refers to *systems*, it includes paying attention to all the systems we are part of and how their dynamics are the subject of our coaching work.

- *Courage* means a willingness to take risks, face our fears, and confront our usual ways of being and behaving.
- *Embodiment* is the ability to be fully present, bringing our head, heart, and guts into the conversation. Embodiment includes identifying somatic indicators that connect the body with specific emotions and implies not ignoring the wisdom of our body and staying centered.

DEVELOPING THE ABILITY TO REGULATE EMOTIONS

The world can be a scary place at times. Regulating our emotions can be challenging because everything happening in the world affects us socially, politically, and economically.

The concept of a volatile, uncertain, complex, and ambiguous world (VUCA) implies the existence of a reality in which we don't find answers and must deal with the fact of living in uncertainty.[5] Living without answers can be incredibly complicated and uncomfortable and can produce emotions that are difficult to navigate, such as anger, sadness, or fear. We all experience these emotions. When leaders with a coaching mindset work with their colleagues, they need to be fully aware of how these emotions are shaping our lives so they don't negatively impact coaching work.

Recently, author and futurist Jamais Cascio spoke of the BANI reality: brittle, anxious, nonlinear, and incomprehensible.[6] The BANI proposal suggests that many of the disruptions we are experiencing disorient, frighten, and stress us because we feel there are no compasses or tools to navigate the challenges.

Brittle

When resources are as fragile as glass, they can easily break, generating fear and insecurity. The illusion of strength can crumble when faced with the unexpected. Fragility can characterize technological, energy, and even political systems, where a failure can unleash chain reactions that are hard to imagine. Just thinking about this can generate anxiety.

Anxious

Anxiety is a state of agitation, restlessness, intense and continuous worry, and excessive fear in everyday situations. Anxiety involves trying to bring the future into the present and expecting everything to be resolved quickly and well. When worry, impatience, or fear interfere with our activities, it becomes a mental disorder. Anxiety carries a sense of helplessness, a fear that whatever we do will be wrong. We are anxious to know what will happen, and when it happens, we find that the novelty quickly becomes obsolete.

Technology accelerates this process. The panic of not being informed about everything minute by minute can lead to paralysis or haste in a world where information overflows, generating more anxiety and greater ignorance.

Nonlinear

We are used to thinking in terms of cause and effect, but we often face phenomena that lack this characteristic, which destabilizes us. Tiny events can have enormous consequences, or an immense gap can occur between the cause and its effect.

COVID-19, climate change and its environmental consequences, and other examples can be found in economics and politics. The disproportionality of the consequences surprises us and either spurs action on our part or leaves us motionless.

Incomprehensible

All the brittleness, anxiousness, and nonlinearities often make these complex situations impossible for us to understand. We witness events that exceed our capacity for understanding based on habitual patterns and internal resources. Obtaining more information does not bring greater clarity and can even lead to more confusion. What seems mysterious today may be clear for us in the long term when we develop new paradigms.

Leaders need to identify their own emotional state and find appropriate mechanisms to process present challenging experiences. They also need to be interested in the emotions of their team members, given the current global political, social, economic, and environmental challenges.

For this reason, leaders who want to develop a coaching mindset may have a coach and explore, reflect, and work on everything that happens to them. What are their emotions? What happens to them when they work with their people? Being able to regulate one's emotions is important for being effective in leadership.

María Inés Gómez, corporate vice president of people and communications at Molymet, has this to say about the benefits of a coaching mindset:

Coaching, in my company, is seen as a powerful tool for leadership development. Personally, I would like more people to have access to coaching. I believe it is good to start developing the potential of people in any position. Achieving this is only a matter of budget and time, but I think it won't take long to implement it because it provides advantages in adapting to the changes emerging in the world. Technology is not enough. It is essential to develop emotional leadership competencies, resilience. Coaching provides a significant space for conversation and reflection, enhances the quality of life and well-being, helps to focus, and reflects on our relationships through dialogues that change our energy and the body.

SEEKING HELP

The ability to ask for help is intimately linked to the ethical elements I discussed in chapter 2. I invite you, as a leader with a coaching mindset prepared to face the challenges posed by the current world, to ensure that you are always assisted by professional coaches who can contribute to your work. From my point of view, executive coaching is a good option.

Francesco Bassoli, vice president of global procurement at Alcoa, talks about the importance of aligning everyone's goals:

When I started in my position as a leader at Alcoa, I asked about goals but not about how to achieve them. I discovered that everyone had goals that were not aligned with the organization and the rest of the team. The company's goals could not be achieved without alignment. I then organized meetings with each of my team members to align goals. In each meeting, we explored the skills needed to achieve what was desired in three years. We also sought to define who we were and who we needed to be. At that moment, for example, the marketing manager was focused on marketing but did not connect with colleagues and did not involve others in the conversation. When we discussed together what his role was, we concluded that it included sharing information, involving people, and listening. We also discussed that for his role to be effective, he had to involve the entire organization in some way and not hesitate to seek help whenever it was deemed necessary. My work plan includes influencing others and being a leader who influences other leaders to engage, participate, and provide coaching to their teams. My management plan also included bringing in an external coach.

MOVING ON

Every society has developed a set of expectations and behaviors that may be quite different from a neighboring society. What is expected and accepted in America's Southern states differs greatly from California or New York City. It is the same with teams in any organization, commercial or nonprofit. Call it your work agreement. But how do leaders develop and share such agreements? We explore that in chapter 4.

CHAPTER SUMMARY

Embodying a coaching mindset entails interacting with team members from a place of appreciation for both who they are and what they can contribute and results. It involves consistently investing time in personal and professional development, both for oneself and for direct reports.

Leaders with a coaching mindset trust that their team members have the necessary capacity to make decisions that positively impact results. Viewing each employee as a whole person with inherent resources and multiple capabilities involves relating as adults and having confidence in their decision-making abilities.

Coaching-minded leaders are open, flexible, and continuous learners. They work with a coach, engage in training, read books, and seek opportunities for daily evolution. They also invest time and energy in the personal and professional growth of their collaborators.

Continuous creation of spaces for reflection, cocreation, and dialogue is necessary to visualize new possibilities for being and doing to inspire and challenge as well as to explore blind spots, ethical dilemmas, and emotional reactions, among other aspects.

A systemic perspective is crucial to avoid blind spots. Coaching-minded leaders need to be aware of the systems they are involved in and constantly question what is happening in their economic, social, and political context. They must be aware that colleagues may be facing multiple personal challenges, to which leaders need to demonstrate empathy, emotional intelligence, and commitment to provide the flexibility needed in our current times.

Nancy Kline presents ten elements to create spaces for reflection: attention, equality, ease, appreciation, encouragement, information, place, incisive questioning, diversity, and feelings.

Coaching-minded leaders need to be clear that they are their own instrument, and their experiences, ideas, emotions, and intuitions constitute a helpful information tool.

Leaders also have to identify their own emotions and find appropriate mechanisms to process their own challenging experiences. Additionally, they should show interest in the emotions of their colleagues.

Whenever possible, leaders need to prepare mentally and emotionally, practice mindfulness or meditation, and take a moment to think or reflect before engaging in a coaching conversation. This centering, along with deep breathing, allows leaders to focus on themselves to change the state of their consciousness.

Similar to how professional coaches are encouraged to seek support, for example, through reflective spaces such as supervision, coaching-minded leaders should ensure they are always assisted by professionals who can contribute to their task.

THE WORK AGREEMENT
CLARIFYING EXPECTATIONS
FOR SUCCESSFUL
RELATIONSHIPS

If there is any one secret of success, it lies in the ability to get the other person's point of view and see things from that person's angle as well as from your own.

— HENRY FORD

All coaching-minded leaders need to be willing to invest time and attention in creating a relationship of trust and transparency with partners. They shouldn't expect team members to read their minds, nor should they assume they know what their partners are thinking or feeling. Good communication creates healthy work environments conducive to building a culture of respect and well-being. In short, a work agreement makes stakeholders comfortable working with each other.

In the era of remote working, leaders understand the pivotal role of communication in volatile, uncertain, complex, and ambiguous times. "Communicate, communicate, communicate" becomes the mantra. More communication is better than less. Colleagues expect clarity from their leaders regarding objectives and what they have to do to achieve those objectives. And communication is not only clearly articulating expectations but also mainly active listening. In the fast world we live in and with the many demands we experience, listening may be challenging.

We will explore communication and listening skills more in chapter 6, but first we'll focus on how to clarify needs and expectations for a foundation of an effective working relationship.

WORK AGREEMENTS

Many times, leaders don't pay enough attention in setting up new relationships for success. Spending time in developing new relationships and clarifying expectations is key in this process. Effective leaders invest time in exploring expectations, clarifying working styles, and articulating mutual needs. For instance, some leaders may not be interested in the intricacies of their collaborators' work, while others want to understand the details of how a result was or will be achieved. Knowing leaders' and collaborators' work preferences fosters an understanding of the similarities and differences in work style methods and helps create optimal working conditions.

Leaders who have developed coaching skills know that setting up the relationship includes investing time in getting to know their new direct reports and colleagues. What is important to them? What are their work preferences? What are their challenges? Ideally, leaders may have collected all this information in the hiring process, but if they are new to a team, it will take time to gather this feedback.

ONBOARDING COACHING FOR NEW EMPLOYEE SUCCESS

The role of a leader is pivotal in shaping the onboarding experience of new employees. A leader's ability to coach and mentor isn't just about imparting knowledge; it's also about cultivating a nurturing atmosphere where new hires feel supported and empowered to bring their best selves to work. Understanding this role is critical to both individual and organizational success.

Leadership during onboarding goes beyond initial orientation. It's about setting the stage for a successful career trajectory within the organization. According to Gallup's report *Creating an Exceptional Onboarding Journey for New Employees* it takes new employees up to twelve months to reach their full performance potential.[1] By offering guidance and support from day one, leaders can significantly shorten this timeline and enhance overall job satisfaction.

KEY STRATEGIES FOR EFFECTIVE ONBOARDING

Here are five key steps leaders should take while onboarding new employees according to Gallup's reports.

Establish Clear Communication

Leaders need to ensure that clear communication lines are established from the outset. This involves clarifying expectations, providing feedback, and being available to answer questions. When new employees understand their roles and responsibilities clearly, they can perform more confidently and competently.

Cultivate a Supportive Environment

Creating an environment where employees feel valued and supported is essential. Leaders need to encourage open dialogue, invite questions, and actively listen to concerns. A supportive environment fosters engagement and encourages new hires to contribute their innovative ideas without fear of judgment.

Encourage Integration into Company Culture

A new employee's integration into the company culture is crucial for long-term retention. Leaders need to facilitate connections between new hires and their colleagues, helping them build relationships that are vital for collaboration and success. This could include arranging meet and greets or assigning mentors who can offer guidance on navigating the organizational culture.

Set Goals and Measure Success for Performance Management

Leaders need to work with new employees to set clear, attainable goals and performance indicators. In doing so, leaders provide a road map for new hires to achieve milestones and measure their progress to manage their performance. Regular check-ins to discuss these goals can help keep employees motivated and aligned with company objectives.

Foster Continuous Learning

Onboarding is not a one-time event but an ongoing process. Leaders need to prioritize continuous learning opportunities, whether through formal training programs or informal knowledge-sharing sessions. Encouraging new employees to learn and grow ensures they remain engaged and invested in their roles.

Here are a few questions the leaders can ask themselves:

- Have I clearly identified and explained the regulations, policies, and procedures my employees need to comply with?
- Have I clearly set employee job expectations and linked them to concrete, time-bound measures?
- Am I supporting my new hires so they will have a full understanding of the company culture?
- Am I connecting with my new employees to establish all the relationships vital to their success?

Onboarding is now even more important as many organizations continue with virtual or hybrid working styles, especially those with international branches.

WORKING IN A HYBRID WORLD

Virtual work has been taking place for several decades as a result of globalization. Teams that meet remotely are characterized by not being physically in the same space and having to collaborate to achieve shared goals.

One of the consequences of the COVID-19 pandemic is a hybrid-work world, with employees having flexible schedules to do some or all of their tasks at home. People have different ideas about how this should be done. Some companies have flexible guidelines, some have closed their physical offices and most work is virtual, and some are once again prioritizing in-person work. Remote work has advantages and disadvantages.

Advantages of Remote Work

Remote work has the advantage of reducing costs, including travel time to meetings, plane tickets, hotels, meals, and parking, among others. Until recently, many leaders believed that if employees did not participate in meetings physically, the quality of work would suffer, and results could be affected. As a consequence, time and money were invested in having team members meet in person as frequently as possible. COVID-19, by forcing remote work, initiated a paradigm shift. Organizations began to realize that they could produce results even when colleagues did not meet in person. This revolutionizes the idea of the need to gather under one roof to achieve results, to the point that many companies, such as Facebook and Google, are offering their employees the option to work from home even when they can return to their offices.

Disadvantages of Remote Work

Employees who don't meet in person may miss opportunities for informal conversations to build trust and develop more intimate working relationships. Additionally, nonverbal communication can be misunderstood, or something unintended may be read between the lines in an email. Furthermore, employees may face technical challenges, such as poor internet service or malfunctioning equipment. The learning curve required for employees to become familiar with the necessary communication tools should also be considered.

STRATEGIES FOR REMOTE WORK

To make the most of remote work, leaders need to take the following seven steps.

Selecting the Right Team Members

Team members need to align with the team's objectives and be motivated to collaborate in a virtual space. The leader needs to identify each colleague's unique needs to thrive in the virtual space and ensure that each is prepared to perform the required tasks. For example, if a participant is uncomfortable or unsure about the technology used to collaborate with colleagues, the leader needs to offer coaching to build confidence or provide training to enable the team member to fulfill the required work.

Promoting Collaboration

It is important for the leader to have clarity and articulate expectations on how each virtual team member collaborates and behaves. Working from home may cause some team members to lose motivation due to a lack of interaction with other colleagues. In this regard, the leader can create opportunities for team members to spend time getting to know each other and understand each other's specific needs.

Minimizing Distractions

Working from home involves interruptions from family members, pets, or others. Perhaps the team member lives near train tracks or an airport, some construction is going on nearby, or the neighbor is mowing the lawn. Workers face many types of interruptions at home that generally do not happen in the office, and team members and leaders need to plan how to navigate these situations. Both the team leader and the leader are responsible for thinking ahead, planning for interruptions, and clarifying and agreeing on how to deal with all these possible distractions.

Establishing Clear Work Norms and Agreements

To keep the virtual team motivated, everyone should be clear about expectations and work methodologies, especially how and when to communicate. Team members and leaders need to come to a consensus on the following questions:

- Is it appropriate to send an email at any time, or should emails and text messages not be sent after a specific time?
- Are there differences between the various forms of communication? For example, can emails be sent but not texts?
- What are the appropriate work boundaries? When working from home, many boundaries between what is and isn't appropriate become blurred. Are team members expected to respond to messages on weekends?
- What example does the leader set?

Understanding the Technology

To keep the team motivated, the technology used must be understood by all its members. Coaching and training need to be carefully planned to ensure that all team members are confident not only in knowing and understanding the software but also in being prepared for possible difficulties, from having no internet connection to issues with video or audio when one doesn't function effectively.

What if some lose their internet connection? Sometimes, people will need to switch from a computer to a phone when the former technology relies on a home connection and the latter operates via satellite.

As much as possible, everyone needs to have more than one computer available at home. This way, when one is not functioning for some reason, the second available one provides the reassurance that other options exist.

Florencia Sabatini, director of communications for Google Latin America, shared her insights on the importance of flexibility and empathy with remote teams:

The pandemic highlighted that leading teams requires a high degree of empathy to navigate challenges. It is important to truly put oneself in the other's shoes. In this stage, those who were not empathetic did not fare well, and neither did their teams. It is necessary to connect more with people, build relationships, show genuine interest, have the ability to revisit objectives continually to prioritize, and be flexible to adapt to contingencies. Developing the necessary muscles to adapt is crucial. Ensuring the tranquility that comes from a good working environment is essential. The environment increasingly conditions performance, and the leader must shape the environment to ensure good performance.

Paying Special Attention to Communication

The digital world forces us to turn our unconscious communication habits into intentional, conscious habits focused on producing results. When working virtually, leaders need to overcommunicate rather than undercommunicate. In other words, they should seek different means for everyone to give and receive information as quickly as possible. Leaders need to pay attention and ensure that all team members are up to date with the information they need. When the information is sensitive, share it in person rather than sending a text or voice message. Both leaders and collaborators need to be clear about the most appropriate methods for sharing different types of messages.

Designing Games and Activities

One way to create teamwork is to share playful activities. Different games require coordination and collaboration and can be played virtually, from Scrabble to charades. Additionally, many remote activities encourage team creativity as well.

Leaders need to avoid underestimating the value of the time when a team plays. These activities provide an opportunity to enjoy a relaxed space and develop personal relationships, encouraging collaboration and coordinated actions. In addition to games, the team can be encouraged to share readings, movies, videos on YouTube, or TED Talks. Doing so creates reflection spaces that may or may not be related to the team's task and responsibilities. Virtual teamwork presents multiple challenges that can be overcome by following the right strategies.

During my experience working with global leaders, I discovered that it is possible to intentionally develop skills, both in leaders and their collaborators, to navigate the challenges of virtuality and achieve expected results. Ultimately, teams need to have clear objectives. Likewise, they must have the clarity to choose the necessary means and operational flexibility that conditions impose.

LONELINESS AT WORK

Gallup's 2024 *State of the Global Workplace* report finds that one in five employees worldwide currently feels lonely at work.[2] As many organizations migrated to remote or virtual workspaces, some leaders began sensing distant staffers were suffering from a kind of remote-office loneliness. That is to say, they missed the informal conversations with colleagues as well as their companionship. They may at first have looked forward to the advantages of a remote workspace: no crawling on the freeway, drinking your own coffee, and so on.

But a coaching-minded leader needs to look out for the downside of virtual loneliness among staff. It can affect productivity. In a *Harvard Business Review* article from 2024, Constance N. Hadley and Sarah L. Wright address the social disconnection at work.[3] They point out that the problems of workplace loneliness persist despite the growing awareness of it. They suggest creating a culture of connection by building socializing into the rhythm of work: offering happy hours, communal lunches, networking programs, well-being initiatives, employee social groups, and off-site activities. The people who reported not feeling lonely said that "their employers offered a frequent and robust set of social opportunities."

When leaders hire new team members, they need to spend time finding out what the new hires need to feel part of the team and connected to the organization. This goes beyond remote workers. When organizations overlook this issue, the level of engagement and sense of belonging may be diminished.

DEVELOPING CULTURAL COMPETENCE

In the previous chapter, I discussed the importance of being aware of culture and context to provide coaching to colleagues on an ongoing basis. Being aware of cultural differences is a part of a coaching mindset and is especially important when we are starting a relationship.

In an increasingly interconnected world, cultural competence is not just a desirable skill but a necessity for effective leadership. Understanding how to operate within a multicultural environment can transform your team's dynamics, foster inclusivity, and enhance your organization's global reach.

We define culture as the integrated pattern of human behavior that includes the thoughts, communication, actions, customs, beliefs, values, and institutions associated with racial, ethnic, religious, or social groups.

Cultural competence involves recognizing, understanding, and valuing diverse cultural backgrounds and perspectives. It requires leaders to adapt their communication and management styles to function effectively across different cultural contexts. By developing these skills, leaders can build stronger relationships with their teams, customers, and stakeholders from varied backgrounds.

Being culturally blind means not being aware of how issues of culture may be affecting the functioning of a team. It may include failing to explore how issues of diversity may negatively affect team members or how some communication styles may be interpreted as disrespectful. It may include discriminatory hiring practices or subtle messages that people of color are not valued or welcome.

Bill Thompson, chief executive officer of Young Storytellers, said,

> The majority of the people on my team are women of color, and this is one of the reasons that motivates me to focus on being more inclusive. I always prefer to listen to others'

ideas before presenting my own. It takes more time, but it's a more effective way to lead. When everyone provides input, the quality of decisions is better. To reinforce this work style, I hired a person to coach all employees.

KEY SKILLS FOR CULTURAL COMPETENCE

The four key skills leaders need to develop cultural competence are discussed below.

Understanding and Valuing Differences

Leaders first need to acknowledge that cultural diversity brings a wealth of ideas and experiences that can drive innovation and growth. This begins by understanding the cultural dimensions that influence people's behavior and values. Recognizing these differences allows leaders to appreciate the unique contributions everyone brings to the table.

Respecting Differences

Respecting cultural differences goes beyond mere acknowledgment; it involves treating others with dignity and fairness. Leaders need to create an environment where all team members feel valued and respected, regardless of their cultural background. This respect fosters trust and collaboration—essential ingredients for a harmonious workplace.

Recognize that the word *respect* keeps showing up in all chapters of this book. It is required to build a relationship, develop trust, and demonstrate ethical leadership.

Showing Interest in Other Cultures

Cultivating a genuine curiosity about other cultures can open doors to deeper understanding and connection. Leaders who show an interest in learning about different customs, traditions, and worldviews demonstrate an openness and willingness to adapt. This curiosity can lead to more meaningful interactions and partnerships.

Leaders need to actively seek opportunities to educate themselves about the cultures they interact with, whether through books, online courses, or cultural immersion experiences. This knowledge can help leaders avoid misunderstandings and communicate more effectively with diverse groups.

Being Sensitive to People from Different Cultures

Cultural sensitivity involves being aware of how your words and actions might be perceived by individuals from different cultural backgrounds. Leaders need to be attuned to nuances and potential cultural misunderstandings and strive to communicate in ways that are inclusive and respectful. This sensitivity can prevent conflicts and reinforce positive relationships. Knowledge about different cultures is not enough. Specific behaviors that foster collaboration and a sense of equity are also necessary.

WHAT CULTURAL COMPETENCE DOES FOR THE TEAM

Cultural competence benefits the team in multiple ways:

- *Enhances team performance*—Culturally competent leaders can harness the diverse talents and perspectives within their team, leading to more creative solutions and improved performance.

- *Improves employee engagement*—When employees feel understood and respected, they are more likely to be engaged and committed to their work.

- *Expands market reach*—Understanding cultural nuances can help businesses tailor their products and marketing strategies to better meet the needs of a global audience.

- *Builds a positive brand image*—Companies known for their cultural competence are often seen as more ethical and socially responsible, which can attract customers and talent.

Developing cultural competence is an ongoing process that requires commitment and effort. By understanding and valuing cultural differences, respecting and showing curiosity about other cultures, and being sensitive to diverse perspectives, leaders can create more inclusive and successful organizations.

COACHING FOR CULTURAL AWARENESS AND RESPECT

I was working with my US-based client Jason and his team who were in long talks with a Japanese firm. A partnership of sorts would enhance both companies. But to Jason's surprise and especially his team's, the negotiations were dragging on, meeting after meeting. Each proposal was met with more deliberations, more consultations, and what seemed like a frustrating lack of urgency to get the deal done. With each proposal, the Japanese team never seemed to offer either positive or negative feedback. Jason and his team members traded bewildering glances. They wondered if this partnership was meant to be.

Jason began to wonder if something cultural was being overlooked, so he brought the issue to explore in our coaching session.

We discussed cultural issues and the possibility that there may be cultural differences in ways of working and expectations between teams. Japanese culture has a tendency to look for collective harmony, and decisions are rarely made by one person; they are reached by consensus of the many, and that takes precedence over speed or deadlines.

After our session, Jason invited the Japanese team for several dinners intended to give them the space to open up and speak first. Smiles became more reassuring. The atmosphere slowly moved from hesitation to trust.

For Jason and his team, it was a big leadership learning experience. The deal got done, and the results exceeded both sides' expectations.

Sometimes, leadership involves stepping out of your own cultural persona and being curious about other cultures. Are you ready to enhance your cultural competence? Start today by exploring new cultures and incorporating these skills into your leadership practice. The impact on your team and organization will be profound and rewarding.

In any collaborative setting, the power of clear agreements cannot be understated. Clarifying roles, responsibilities, and expectations creates a bedrock of trust and accountability. Without this clarity, misunderstandings and conflicts can easily arise, sapping energy and undermining productivity. By taking the time to outline agreements from the beginning, teams craft a shared road map that aligns everyone toward common goals, fostering a sense of unity and purpose.

Clear agreements do more than just set expectations; they empower everyone to take ownership of their role and contribute meaningfully. When challenges emerge, having a framework of established agreements makes it easier to address and resolve conflicts constructively. This proactive stance not only boosts collaboration but also nurtures a culture of transparency and mutual respect.

Dedicating time to establish clear agreements upfront is an investment in building resilient teams that can weather adversity and thrive together.

MOVING ON

Did you ever have a boss you were skeptical about? Maybe they made uncertain, sometimes inappropriate comments about other people or management. Deep inside, you felt that something wasn't right. Trust is a characteristic often tarnished by such intuition. Now that you know how important trust is as you become a leader with a coaching mindset, read on.

CHAPTER SUMMARY

Leaders with a coaching mindset establish clear work agreements with their team members under the belief that exploring expectations increases effectiveness and reduces misunderstandings.

Leaders understand the crucial role of communication in volatile, uncertain, complex, and ambiguous times. Clear communication is essential to provide clarity on objectives and expectations for employees. Lack of clarity in assessing success parameters leads to confusion and inadequate resource utilization.

Tools for self-awareness and awareness development enable conversations focused on leveraging strengths as well as addressing opportunities.

Key strategies for effective onboarding include establishing clear communication, cultivating a supportive environment, encouraging integration into company culture, setting goals and measuring success for performance management, and fostering continuous learning.

A leader with a coaching mindset must understand—and manage—the pros and cons of remote working arrangements. Working remotely can be a shock to the system for some, even though they may at first have looked forward to its advantages, such as no more driving to work. A big disadvantage is remote loneliness and the lack of in-person socializing. A leader must understand and recognize the advantages of remote versus hybrid versus traditional office environments.

Key skills for cultural competence include understanding and valuing differences, respecting differences, showing interest in other cultures, and being sensitive to people from different cultures.

Cultural competence enhances team performance, improves employee engagement, and strengthens work relationships.

CULTIVATING TRUST
A PROCESS THAT CANNOT
BE OVERLOOKED

As a manager, you may give orders, but as a
leader of choice, trust is a requirement to be taken
seriously as a coach.

—DAMIÁN GOLDVARG

Trust is the foundation of any coaching relationship. In fact, in any successful relationship, personal or professional, cultivating trust and a safe place is key to having supportive and challenging conversations. When trust exists, colleagues feel valued and have confidence in their leader. This requires time and intentional effort and cannot be taken for granted.

This chapter explores strategies for building trust. We will cover the five types of trust you will need to develop in yourself as a leader, as a coach, in your team members, in the coaching process, and in the organization. Later, we'll discuss the four key elements identified by Stephen M. R. Covey in *The Speed of Trust*: integrity, intent, capabilities, and results.[1]

As we discussed in chapter 2 on ethical leadership, you can build high levels of trust by demonstrating integrity. Are you treating your direct reports as valuable humans who require support and development? Are you investing time in clear communication? Are you deeply listening to their concerns? Trust fosters satisfying and engaging work relationships and creates healthy and potentially prosperous workspaces that encourage creativity, expanded thinking, alignment, and better outcomes— financially and emotionally.

Leaders need to remember that trust, built over time, even years, can be lost if neglected. Therefore, coaching-minded leaders consistently strive to develop healthy work relationships, showing respect for direct reports and collaborators. Above all, they make every effort to support, acknowledge, and develop their team and not disappoint them.

A PERSONAL STORY OF DISAPPOINTMENT

In 2002, I worked at Personnel Decisions International offering leadership development programs involving coaching, training, and assessment centers worldwide. I had a learning experience that was painful but also taught me a good lesson.

I had two bosses, one for my local work in Los Angeles and another one for my work in Latin America. On one occasion, I started offering services to a Latin American company through my local office and forgot to let my Latin American leader know. When she found out, she was upset with me for not keeping her informed. She claimed it made her look bad with her own boss and told me she felt she could not trust me any longer.

I remember how painful the experience was. Even though my behavior had been unintentional, I had to work hard to regain her trust. I learned that doing so was possible, but it required effort and perseverance to keep her informed of all my work. Consistent behavior is what enhances trust. In this situation, a simple "For your information," or FYI, note might have prevented the difficult situation.

TIMES ARE CHANGING

Building trust in an organization has become more important than ever given virtual work arrangements. Leaders need to continually monitor the level of trust.

The Edelman Trust Barometer is an annual survey conducted by Edelman, a global communications firm, which measures trust and credibility across various institutions, sectors, and geographies.[2] It provides insights into how trust in governments, businesses, nongovernmental organizations, and media evolves over time and highlights key trends and factors influencing public trust.

The 2024 Edelman report shows a decline in trust toward leaders, with 61 percent of respondents believing that business leaders are purposely trying to mislead people, saying things they know are false or exaggerated.

Trust in business leaders depends on their perceived competence and ethical behavior. Leaders that demonstrate these qualities can receive higher levels of trust from their employees and the public.

To build and maintain trust, the Edelman report suggests that leaders would focus on four key areas:

- *Transparency*—Have clear communication and be open about challenges and mistakes.
- *Engagement*—Listen to and address concerns.
- *Ethical conduct*—Demonstrate integrity and follow the organization's values.
- *Collaboration*—Partner with stakeholders to foster a sense of collective effort and shared responsibility.

STRATEGIES FOR BUILDING TRUST

Effective leaders adopt the following strategies to build team trust.

Invest Energy in Getting to Know Team Members

Our company, Goldvarg Consulting Group, has been training leaders worldwide in coaching and effective communication skills since the year 2000. One of the initial exercises in our leadership program involves participants identifying a leader they have worked with and admire. They create a list highlighting the behaviors and attitudes that set this leader apart and make them an extraordinary leader.

Consistently, participants in our programs identify trust as a key element in their relationship with leaders. When asked about the factors contributing to this trust, they assert that their leaders showed interest in them not only as producers of results but also as individuals with specific needs, unique values, and dreams for the future.

Here is a question for you: to put it bluntly, do your people feel they are chess pieces needed for your success, or do they feel seen as human beings doing their best possible work? Go through the staff names and consider each person's likely response.

Admired leaders are familiar with the personal lives of their direct reports and show interest in their activities outside of work and in their families. In other words, standout leaders genuinely commit to getting to know their employees beyond the workplace. They consider this information whenever possible when providing flexibility in projects and aligning personal values and interests with those of the organization. Leaders understand that if they can align their team member roles as much as possible with what ignites and motivates them, they will inspire employees to be engaged and do what is required because it provides meaning and energy.

One of my clients shared a story about an assistant who was unmotivated. She had a car accident and had some lingering physical pain. She also did not find any interest in her work. My client had a conversation to identify what her passions were, what she cared about, and what was important to her to find ways to align these to her work. It took some exploration to uncover the assistant was intrigued about becoming a physical therapist since she had a positive experience working with one as a result of her accident.

My client supported her in learning about the field, finding a school to get training, and providing flexibility to accommodate her training. As a result, this assistant became the best one she ever had. By supporting her in what was important to her, even though it was not directly related to her work, she was able to get the best from her. Eventually, the assistant got a job as a physical therapist. My client had to find a new assistant to replace the most motivated one she ever had.

Understanding and knowing team members does not necessarily mean sharing their beliefs or values. It simply entails comprehending their sources of motivation and interest. This information is then utilized when making decisions or delegating tasks. Showing genuine interest in others is one of the most effective ways to build trust, sending the message "I want to know you and understand you to help you be more effective and achieve your personal and organizational goals."

When leaders are aware of each team member's context, they have information that enables them to understand factors that may affect performance. For example, if a team member is not focused at work, and the leader knows that they or their family member is facing a health issue, being attentive becomes easier. The leader can offer flexibility and support instead of becoming upset. By being flexible within the realm of possibility and seeking creative ways to meet the employee's needs, leaders increase trust. They are perceived as fair colleagues who support not only the organization and team needs but also the individual needs of each team member. It is a win-win outcome for all involved.

Respect Team Members

Knowing and respecting team members are complementary behaviors. Each team member is different. Invest time in getting to know them and adapt their coaching to the specific needs of each individual. This requires intentionality—dedicating time, attention, active interest, and flexibility.

Why is intentionality important? Because leaders need to consciously invest time, energy, and effort in identifying their direct reports' expectations, needs, strengths, and areas of development.

Flexibility is necessary because coaching cannot be delivered to all team members in the same way. Trustworthy leaders tailor the language, style, and tone to each person to the extent possible.

Respecting team members means understanding their communication preferences, drivers of behavior, and motivation. For example, some of your team might prefer more freedom and independence in their tasks, while others need more collaboration and guidance, feeling more secure when they know you are always available for consultation. Some members value receiving recognition publicly, while others feel embarrassed by it.

Leaders who consistently respect their team members communicate to them in a cordial, professional tone, regardless of being stressed, tired, or in a bad mood. They don't lose their ability to be kind in tense situations. This may seem like a significant demand, almost superhuman. But when leaders have good working relationships, their team members, as a result of trust, can understand that the leaders are overwhelmed when they struggle to maintain composure in high-stress situations.

Leaders who are committed to unleashing their direct reports' potential are aware of the importance of making each team member feel valued, irrespective of gender, religion, age, or sexual orientation. Leaders who respect their team members not only avoid making ironic, sarcastic, or offensive comments but also pay attention to any of these types of comments made by others in the team.

If that happens, they don't stay silent; they intervene, explaining that such comments have no place on their team. Coaching-minded leaders understand that team members may have different communication styles or cultural diversities that can influence communication, so they make an effort to understand how these differences can be gracefully overcome.

Be Empathetic

Empathy—another critical skill to build trust—is the ability to demonstrate understanding of others' experiences, beliefs, and emotions. You don't need to have had identical experiences to identify with someone else's situation or emotions. However, the intention to "put oneself in their shoes," to reflect on the possible meaning of the other person's experience, fosters empathy and connection and leads to building trust.

Suppose a team member goes through a stressful situation with a client. You could ask questions to help them learn from the experience, validate or normalize if appropriate, and share your personal experience with a similar client. Even if you haven't had the same experience, an empathic approach involves asking questions to understand what the team member is going through and what it might mean for them in a way that builds connection. This perception of understanding enables effective support, openness, and respect.

In another example, a leader who is single and has on her team a mother who needs flexibility to take her kids to school may not have the experience of being a parent. They can still be understanding, supportive, and caring and show flexibility toward their team member.

The discovery of the mirror neuron system has shed light on various aspects of empathy.[3] Our mirror neurons embody the actions, sensations, and emotions of others, allowing us as humans to embody them through mimicry and social contagion. This system facilitates putting ourselves in another person's place, even anticipating and deducing someone's intentions before they turn into actions. For example, if we see someone cry, mirror neurons can make us cry and thus experience a sensation similar to what the other person is feeling.

Coaching-minded leaders demonstrate empathy when perceiving or inferring the feelings, thoughts, and emotions of others, using this information to understand their team members from their perspective rather than from the leaders' perspective or indirectly experiencing their team members' feelings and perceptions. Coaching-minded leaders also attentively listen to the concerns of their direct reports to understand their experiences and challenges to be able to be more supportive.

During a coaching session, a leader shared with me that two direct reports on his team, leaders of their own teams, had conflicts resulting from different perspectives on priorities and methodologies. They couldn't agree on several operational issues. When I interviewed the team members, one told me that their leader didn't understand them and that they didn't feel supported. As a result, they felt they couldn't trust the leader to provide the assistance required to achieve the expected goals. This created distance and resentment between the two team members with the leader.

In our coaching session, we met with the leader and two team members and explored the situation. The leader asked questions and demonstrated interest in understanding everyone's perspective. By showing empathy and understanding, he was able to start rebuilding trust. Consequently, everyone could work more effectively with each other and achieve the desired results.

Fernando Perla, the technology manager at Banco Santander shared these thoughts on leadership empathy:

Being empathetic goes beyond surface-level information, getting closer to team members, making them feel that we share their responsibilities. For example, we had trouble implementing a critical system. We discovered a significant flaw that needed immediate repair. It was six in the evening, the end of the workday. The person who had to fix the error said it would take at least a week.

The problem was that we needed the result by the next day. I sensed there was more to the problem, so I asked the person what was preventing them from completing the task sooner. Their response was "If I make a mistake, I could lose my job." My obvious reply was, "I take responsibility for whatever may happen if we make a mistake."

As a result, we stayed and worked hard, and the job was completed late that evening. I believe the reassurance my support provided helped bring out the best in them and fulfill the objective. Many times, I've found that problems that seem to have a purely technical background involve human, team, or political factors hidden behind technological impossibilities as in this case.

The celebrated author and professor Brené Brown argues that empathy is necessary to create organizational cultures with connection and trust.[4] She differentiates empathy from sympathy, defining the former as "feeling with" and the latter as "feeling for." Brown outlines four skills to develop empathy:

- *See the world from others' perspectives*—While we may not be able to remove our own lenses shaped by education, parental influence, and teachers, we can honor perspectives different from ours. Taking into account other perspectives requires listening and behaving like a learner rather than an expert, demonstrating genuine interest.
- *Withhold judgment*—Based on Brown's research, we know that we judge others when we feel susceptible to shame or when others do something worse than us in the same areas. We need to be aware of our own internal struggles with what embarrasses us.
- *Understand people's feelings and communicate understanding*—To fully understand others, we need to recognize our own feelings and be emotionally literate. This means having a broad vocabulary to choose the word that best expresses what we feel. Without the right words to articulate our emotions, it becomes hard to process them effectively.
- *Mindfulness*—We pay attention to what is happening during each conversation. We take into account our own emotional and physical reactions, as well as the interlocutor's body language. We try to maintain balance and not minimize or exaggerate responses.

Bill Thompson, CEO of Young Storytellers, says the following about communication practices:

> In my team, everyone gives and receives feedback. This builds trust and fairness. I meet one-on-one with team members and take the opportunity to ask and give them a chance to be heard. I aim to convey the message that they are a priority for me. When someone has ideas, I implement them and put my best effort into making them successful. This way, there are more possibilities for everyone to share their ideas on how to do things in the best possible way.

Demonstrate Openness, Transparency, and Vulnerability

To build trust, leaders need to show interest in the ideas of their team members, even if they disagree. Being open to different perspectives is necessary to create a work environment that values differences and new thinking. This also means sharing as much information as possible appropriately to create transparency. It may prevent others from believing the information is being manipulated as well.

Leaders who are vulnerable are willing to share information and experiences from a place of authenticity, allowing them to be seen as a human with strengths and weaknesses, which creates a deeper level of connection.

Vulnerability is not weakness but quite the opposite. Weakness implies feeling incapable or lacking the strength required to face a situation. In this context, vulnerability is related to authenticity; we show our humanity and embrace our imperfections instead of being ashamed of them. Leaders who are willing to be vulnerable know they don't know everything and can make errors.

When leaders relate to others from a place of humanity, they achieve higher levels of closeness, loyalty, and commitment. To share beliefs and feelings honestly, even if these are embarrassing us, requires courage and taking risks because leaders don't know how they will be interpreted. However, they do know that they are acting with authenticity and transparency, becoming role models to their collaborators.

Leaders who acknowledge their mistakes instead of presenting themselves as a superhero without any flaws allow people to see their own humanity. Trust is intimately linked to transparency, creating a professional and personal connection, sharing personal experiences, and clarifying the agenda and expectations.

Francesco Bassoli, vice president of global procurement of Alcoa, says, "I joined the company to implement best practices. I listen to my people as much as I speak. I seek to have an authentic, two-way conversation, asking questions and listening carefully to the answers. I provide feedback whenever necessary and consistently work on connecting with my colleagues."

BRAVING

Brené Brown identifies seven elements in the "anatomy of trust" and groups them into the acronym BRAVING:[5]

> *Boundaries*—Have clear boundaries and understand what is and is not appropriate for oneself and why. It involves the ability to say no.

Reliability—Be consistent in delivering on promises. It implies understanding one's competencies and circumstances, ensuring not to promise what cannot be fulfilled.

Accountability—Respect agreements, acknowledge mistakes, apologize, and make amends when necessary.

Vault—Maintain confidentiality, and don't share information that should not be disclosed.

Integrity—Choose courage over comfort, picking what is right over what is fast, fun, or easy. Practice values rather than just talk about them.

Nonjudgment—Be able to ask for what is needed without self-judgment.

Generosity—Have a generous interpretation of others' intentions, words, and actions.

Coaching-minded leaders need to cultivate all the elements of BRAVING to address the challenges faced by their direct reports.

FIVE TYPES OF TRUST

From my personal experience of working with leaders for more than thirty years, I believe leaders of choice, who are committed to developing their team members, demonstrate five types of trust:

- Trust in oneself as a leader
- Trust in oneself as a coach

- Trust in the team members
- Trust in the coaching process
- Trust in the organization

Trust in Oneself as a Leader

Leaders with a coaching mindset strive to do the best possible job and trust in their abilities. When coaching leaders, I like to ask them, "Have you done the best possible job? Have you invested all available energy?" This leads to conversations exploring their level of personal investment in decision-making and their belief in having the capacity to do the best they can.

Having confidence in oneself means believing that we can be successful not only in doing a specific job but also at inspiring and developing others. It requires self-awareness, confidence, and commitment to continuous learning. If the leaders are confident in themselves, they will not fear the development of team members who could potentially compete with them for future jobs or even become their bosses.

Trust in Oneself as a Coach

When leaders lack experience in coaching their team members, they may not feel confident in how to do it effectively. Like any new skill, this requires a time investment for development.

Dedicating time to coach direct reports is not common practice for many leaders. They may prioritize other activities, leave matters related to the development of their team at the end of their to-do list, and coach only if they have spare time. This common attitude generally has a negative impact on the business. When people don't believe they are heard and valued, they can become disengaged and not work as effectively as they could.

Gallup's *State of the Global Workplace* report shows that leaders who invest in coaching achieve greater results and commitment.[6]

Trust in the Team Members

Team members are, in most cases, at different levels of skill, capacity, knowledge, and experience. Some have worked to know themselves in personal growth workshops, with psychologists, coaches, or mentors, or by reading self-help books, while others have not.

To develop an effective relationship, leaders need to trust their direct reports, believe that they are prepared for the job or have the required capacity to develop necessary skills, and trust that they are committed to doing the best possible job. In some cases, this is not the reality. A question I pose during my coaching sessions is, "What do you need to trust in your team or team members?"

Trust in the Coaching Process

Coaching-minded leaders know that coaching works because they have seen the results of their own work. They have seen how colleagues increase their commitment, responsibility, and results. Therefore, leaders have confidence in the coaching process and know it produces desired outcomes. Sometimes, it may take longer than expected and, when it does not work, it may mean a team member has a performance problem that may require a more direct approach. This belief encourages leaders to invest time and energy in working for the personal and professional improvement of their direct reports.

Trust in the Organization

The leaders with a coaching mindset know that results will be dependent not only on the commitment from their team members to do the best possible job but also on the support of the organization. They need to believe that the organization is interested and supports all its employees, including themselves as leaders, as well as their team's well-being. The organization's stakeholders include all its leaders (every team member), the CEO, the board, and any other parties, depending on the organization.

Florencia Sabatini, director of communication at Google Latin America, shares the importance of a leader's intuition and initiative:

> I use my intuition, and if I see someone struggling, I worry. I start to investigate. For example, I don't like seeing someone overloaded with work. I can't ignore that. A good leader is intuitive and trusts their intuition and investigates. When I address an issue that concerns a team member before they bring it up, I know I gain their trust. This is one reason why I try to be attentive, even where I am not there in person. I care about understanding what is happening and protecting each team member.

COVEY'S FOUR STRATEGIES FOR TRUST DEVELOPMENT

The Speed of Trust is a seminal book that for twenty years has offered one of the most well-known models linking trust to leadership. Stephen M. R. Covey identified four key elements for building trust that can be applied to leaders when coaching their direct reports: integrity, intention, capability, and results.[7] These concepts stand the test of time and conclude our discussion on trust.

Integrity

The first element, integrity, was explained in chapter 2 on ethical leadership. It refers to the consistency between what is said and what is done. For example, if leaders promise their team members a raise or something they cannot deliver, the result is a loss of credibility and trust. In the future, team members may doubt their leader's promises.

This problem often occurs when leaders have good intentions, but for reasons they cannot control, the good results do not materialize. As a result, the team's level of trust in their leaders decreases. Therefore, leaders must be clear that they cannot commit to things they cannot fulfill, as regaining trust takes time and energy, and it is not always possible.

Lack of integrity is the easiest and quickest way to lose trust. If trust does not exist, leaders need to invest time in cultivating it because coaching is not possible without the appropriate level of trust. Leaders may have enough authority for direct reports to follow their instructions, but without trust, they will not gain the commitment, motivation, and loyalty that indicate full confidence from the team.

Since coaching is based on the development of the person being coached, integrity is a requirement in the process of coaching conversations to build trust between parties. The congruence that characterizes integrity is not only necessary between what is said and what is done but also between the actions that the leader takes and how their values are demonstrated. Covey includes humility as a key component of integrity.

Intention

Leaders with a coaching mindset clearly express their intentions, meaning their vision and objectives, and don't expect their colleagues to read their mind. When leaders clarify their expectations, misunderstandings are avoided, and a relationship based on clear guidelines is developed, leaving no room for surprises.

When providing coaching to leaders, I find that they often struggle to articulate their expectations and hope team members make decisions aligned with organizational strategies without providing necessary information. In one case, a director was upset with a manager responsible for opening a store because they did not follow certain corporate guidelines. However, during our coaching session, the director realized that they had not been specific in articulating their expectations and asking the team member to follow corporate guidelines.

Many organizational conflicts are based on attributing wrong intentions, either from the leader to the employee or from the employee to the leader. Greater transparency and vulnerability from the leader together with clarity around expectations can reduce the possibility of misunderstandings and unnecessary conflicts.

Capability

Capability includes knowledge, skills, abilities, talent, and personal style. If a leader continuously works on their professional development, they are perceived as credible. Leaders demonstrating coaching skills share everything they learn daily with their team members and support them to continue developing their competencies.

Effective leaders in building trust invest time in developing their skills as both a leader and a coach. They work with their own coach in continuous development to ensure they have the necessary capacity to respond to their responsibilities, both current and future. This way, they become role models for others.

Results

When a leader achieves results, trust is generated, and when team members produce results, trust is reciprocally reinforced. Acknowledgments, feedback, and celebrations of results also help to build trust.

Building trust is a key competence for coaching-minded leaders. Leaders need to pay attention to the level of trust they have built with their team members and intentionally invest time to cultivate all relationships. By paying attention to the level of trust, leaders may be able to intentionally spend time in demonstrating behaviors that reinforce their commitment to the development of their teams.

By involving the team in decision-making and demonstrating genuine concern for their well-being, leaders create a shared environment where team members feel they cocreate a favorable workspace, allowing them to give their best and contribute to the organization. Consequently, team members are engaged, feel secure and valued, and are guided to maximize their potential.

MOVING ON

Can you recall a time when you were with a colleague who appeared to be off in space someplace else? Maybe this person had fidgety body language, darting eyes, or overall wasn't really listening. Obviously, something was not right. Maybe the colleague was preoccupied. Now imagine a boss like that. You would leave an encounter with that boss wondering if you were in trouble. Or he with his boss. Either way, such behavior is a big distraction. A leader with a coaching mindset is always in the here and now—attentive, undistracted. It's called *presence*, and that's the next topic.

CHAPTER SUMMARY

Trust is cultivated over time and requires investment, intention, and effort and should not be taken for granted. It may take a long time to develop and a short time to lose. Without trust, coaching another is not possible.

Leaders with a coaching mindset support their direct reports to cocreate a favorable work environment to give their best and contribute to the organization.

Edelman suggests that leaders focus on four areas: transparency, engagement, ethical conduct, and collaboration.

Brené Brown emphasizes the importance of empathy in creating organizational cultures with connection and trust, distinguishing between empathy (feeling with) and sympathy (feeling for). Developing empathy involves understanding others' perspectives, adopting a nonjudgmental mindset, understanding and communicating feelings, and practicing mindfulness.

Strategies to build trust include investing energy to get to know team members beyond the workplace, respecting individual differences, being empathetic, and demonstrating openness, transparency, and vulnerability.

Brené Brown identifies seven elements in the anatomy of trust using the acronym BRAVING: boundaries, reliability, accountability, vault, integrity, nonjudgment, and generosity.

Leaders with a coaching mindset develop five types of trust: in themselves as a leader, in themselves as a coach, in the team members, in the coaching process, and in the organization.

In *The Speed of Trust*, Stephen M. R. Covey identifies four key elements for trust development: integrity (consistency between words and actions), intention (developing a relationship based on clear guidelines), capability (including knowledge, skills, abilities, talent, and personal style), and results (achieving results generates trust downward and upward).

THE PRESENT LEADER
LOCKING YOUR MIND IN
THE HERE AND NOW

The ability to be in the present moment is a key
component of mental health.

—ABRAHAM MASLOW

We expect our leaders to be attentive to us and to remain
focused during our time with them. This requires us to
be fully aware, respond in the here and now, and limit unrelated
dialogue and thoughts about the past or future or any other distractions. We cannot listen, demonstrate understanding, or be
empathetic without being fully present.

Presence is a multipurpose term that can describe one's mere
location or, as I use it in this chapter, how others perceive us as
being attentive to them. We often use the term *leadership presence* to describe a confidence or comfort with authority, but I use

the term here to describe something closer to mindfulness and focus in relation to others.

The constant bombardment of information, the complexity of the situations we face, and their ambiguity all make attaining leadership presence challenging. However, maintaining presence is crucial to exercise effective leadership.

To obtain a professional coaching certification with ICF, every coach must demonstrate competence in "maintaining presence."[1] Leaders need to do the same! Paying attention to our staff members and colleagues and establishing deep connections with them demonstrates our commitment to the quality of relationships.

The ICF also indicates that using an "open, flexible, and safe style" demonstrates presence as a coach. In your organization, being present probably means that you must have the capacity to adapt quickly to the different scenarios presented by team members, which can sometimes be entirely novel and unexpected. This involves, when appropriate, letting go of limiting beliefs, perspectives, or previous hypotheses that may restrict understanding of the matter being worked on right now.

A FORMER STAR EMPLOYEE

A client shared a sobering experience about losing a highly effective team member due to unintentional neglect. This star employee felt overlooked as my client focused more on team members facing performance challenges. Despite the high performer's request for more challenging assignments, the leader failed to meet his needs. Instead of seeking opportunities to delegate tasks and mentor this talented individual, my client inadvertently drove him away.

Don't let this happen to you. The departure of this key player had a ripple effect, negatively impacting the organization, the team, and the leader himself, who had to shoulder the extra workload until a replacement was found. This experience underscores a vital lesson for leaders: by being present and attentive to the needs of all employees, not just those struggling, leaders can foster a more effective and engaged team, ultimately enhancing retention and development.

Having an open attitude includes being willing to explore unknown territories. It includes being comfortable with discomfort and being willing to change perspectives in the face of uncertainty or lack of knowledge, without losing sight of the goal.

Flexibility is one of the most important attitudes for dealing with challenges.

One interesting story from *Fast Company* years ago talked about John Mackey, CEO of Whole Foods Market, who was confronted by an animal-rights activist during a shareholder meeting.[2] The activist criticized the treatment of ducks supplied to Whole Foods, highlighting concerns about animal welfare within the company's supply chain. Mackey took the activist's concerns seriously and agreed to investigate the matter, which led to company-wide changes in their animal welfare policies.

All coaching competencies presented in this book are closely related to each other. Presence, for example, is closely related to trust and active listening, which will be covered in the next chapter. Presence builds trust. When leaders are present, team members feel connected to their leader, predisposing them to listen and share their own emotions and concerns.

BEHAVIORS THAT DEMONSTRATE PRESENCE

When leaders are present, they are focused, empathetic, and receptive to each team member. Given that one of the key tasks of coaching-minded leaders is to contribute to the learning and growth of their team members, connecting with each team member is required. This involves paying attention to the here and now. Maintaining this type of presence brings people closer. For example, leaders may invite their team members to share how they are doing and feeling when they arrive for a meeting, including what is on their minds that they need to let go to be present in the session.

When I train leaders on coaching skills as well as professional coaches, I often start my sessions with an exercise inviting participants to pay attention to their breathing, somatic experiences, emotions, and thoughts. I also ask them to let go of any thoughts that may be in their way during the session so they can concentrate and be more present during the class.

Staying present requires the leader to develop a level of awareness that enables them, when meeting with team members, to consider everything that is happening based on multiple sources of information they receive:

- What the team member is saying, which requires the ability to listen to others
- What they are saying to themselves, which requires the ability to listen to their inner voice
- What the context is saying, which involves paying attention to how economic, social, and political events affect the situation

In *The Power of Now*, Eckhart Tolle refers to the importance of the concept of mindfulness, which can be understood as a "fully concentrated mind" or "pure presence."[3] He explains the significance of letting go of thoughts that prevent us from being present in different situations. Concentration and breathing play an important role in this.

Mindfulness has its roots in Buddhism and is used in meditation to dispel distractions and focus on a mantra or breathing. Its application aims to achieve awareness of the present, accepting it while setting aside judgments and desires.

MINDFULNESS MASTERY

Mastery of mindfulness involves focus, a state in which one is alert and relaxed simultaneously, achieved through intention. It includes the ability to concentrate, patience, and compassion for oneself and others. There is a connection between this practice and techniques that focus on the here and now. It requires slowing down our attention to recognize our own experiences and those of others, such as noticing a sigh, an anxious movement of the feet or fingers, the rhythm of breathing, and the images that arise during conversation.

In his book *The Mindful Coach*, Doug Silsbee writes that "the ability to be present is an internal state that can be developed."[4] This author argues that there are three gateways to presence: the body, the mind (what we think about or focus on), and the heart, with its emotions.

Alexis Ekizian, head of midmarket sales at Google SpLatam in Buenos Aires, Argentina, says, "During conversations, I pay attention to body language, give team members time to elaborate, and encourage avoiding multitasking. I emphasize that everyone should be present. I try to practice mindfulness more regularly, aiming to create a culture of pause. I also promote the use of breathing techniques, meditation, and yoga, prioritizing the well-being of my team."

Silsbee explains in his book that "mindfulness is a state of presence in which we are aware of our feelings and thoughts, and the habits of our mind, and we can let go of those that do not help us, so they do not limit us." The author maintains that cultivating mindfulness is a lifelong process that requires letting go of our habitual ways of judging the world and understanding our relationships to create new forms of interpretation and connection.

According to Silsbee, being present can allow you to be more effective in life, be more creative, deal with challenges more effectively, respond more agilely, and demonstrate greater authenticity. Being present provides more resources to face life's circumstances. This possibility is always available; one just needs to realize that access is possible.

One of many opportunities for leaders to show presence is under conflict or stress. When leaders face challenges and are present and centered, they have an easier time navigating what is in front of them. Showing presence may require breathing and self-talk about paying attention to their body, emotions, and thoughts that may be hindering the experience.

Adopting the state of presence means being fully aware of the context and prepared to face whatever appears, using all available resources for this purpose. Being present involves listening deeply and having the essential openness to transcend preconceived ideas that give meaning to our reality.

Silsbee defines presence as "a state of consciousness characterized by being an experience of complete surrender." Those who are present are not controlling the clock. They establish a connection with their inner selves and those around them. They reduce their internal dialogue. Presence implies awakening. It allows dealing with stress.

In the book *Presence-Based Leadership*, Silsbee suggests that in complex situations, leaders need to take the following steps:[5]

- Recognize and accept the complexity of the external context.
- Develop a language with new distinctions that allow them to observe themselves and the world from a new place.
- Explore situations from multiple perspectives and find new meanings.
- Acquire new competencies instead of sticking with the skills they already have.
- Cultivate presence, resilience, and equanimity.

Chade-Meng Tan, one of the pioneers in applying mindfulness in companies, teaches that this practice leads to developing a mind capable of maintaining calm and clarity through the training of two faculties: attention and meta-attention, which is the ability to pay attention to our own attention.[6]

Meng, as he likes to be known, worked with Google personnel to teach the usefulness of meditation and practicing mindfulness in other daily practices, such as conversation and even eating. Through a mindfulness practice that is based on paying attention to breathing, distractions, concerns, and judgments are avoided. This results in a state of calm and concentration, translating into a significant reduction in stress and an equally significant increase in overall well-being. The author also teaches that when distractions appear, they should be recognized—but not as a reason for self-criticism—and released so they leave in the same way they appeared.

As mindfulness develops, one becomes more present, capturing the here and now more intensely, and ceases to live mechanically. At the same time, letting go of judgments frees up energy suitable for cultivating patience and compassion, which work in favor of relationships with others and oneself. A growing number of leaders use breathing and meditation as tools and apply mindfulness to their leadership style.

DEMONSTRATING INTEREST

When you are present, you will be curious and genuinely interested in understanding your direct reports. Do you ask them why they behave as they do? What makes them successful? Are there factors that limit them from unleashing their full potential when producing results? What are their fears? What do they value? What is their preferred way to produce results?

Genuine curiosity made a difference between leaders who are close to their team members and those who distance themselves. The investment they did or didn't make left traces that are still visible. The current times require leaders who are eager to understand the unique challenges of their team members and the ability to align individual, team, and organizational needs.

THE DANGER OF NOT KNOWING
WHAT YOU DON'T KNOW

The curiosity inherent in coaching-minded leaders makes them refrain from rushing to conclusions. They ask questions to understand—lots of questions. They know that they may have blind spots, things they are not seeing. This curiosity reminds them that they don't know what they don't know (blind spots), a distinction used often in professional coaching because it defines the scope of what is and isn't possible for the client.

Fernando Perla, the technology manager at Banco Santander, says, "Curiosity is important for us. Two soft skills we seek are being curious and communicative. A coaching-minded leader is empathetic, prioritizes what is important and impactful, and is present, attentive to both spoken and unspoken aspects. There is much left unsaid in meetings that can be adapted to emerging needs. Curiosity is crucial because a coaching-minded leader needs to keep learning all the time; that's why I seek continuous learning opportunities."

In their organizational work, present leaders are aware of their blind spots, and they acknowledge that their team members experience the same. This is the reason they actively work to identify these blind spots and prevent them from hindering the achievement of optimal results.

Bill Thompson, CEO of Young Storytellers, shares the importance of mindfulness: "When I am coaching my team members all my focus is on them. I pay attention to their body language, to what they say and what they don't say. It's a task that can be tiring at times. Being present requires a great deal of energy, but coaching is about being in service to each person."

MOVING ON

Recall for a moment colleagues who always seemed to understand you. How did they listen, not just with their ears but also with their entire self. We live in times in which multitasking is praised as a wonderful ability. But being present in the here and now, having a coaching mindset as a leader, requires a deeper type of listening. That's the next chapter.

CHAPTER SUMMARY

The constant bombardment of information, the complexity of situations today, and their ambiguity make it challenging to stay in the present during each conversation.

Leaders embodying a coaching mindset need to be present to connect effectively with their team members. This involves being fully aware, focusing on the here and now, and identifying and limiting internal dialogue and thoughts about the past, future, or other distractions during conversations.

Using an open, flexible, and secure style means leaders have the capacity to adapt to different scenarios presented by colleagues, setting aside personal beliefs, perspectives, or prior assumptions that may limit their understanding of the discussed matter. This attitude demonstrates confidence in oneself and the coaching process. Having an open attitude includes a willingness to explore unknown topics and being comfortable with discomfort when faced with unknowns or the need to change perspectives.

Staying present requires the leader to be aware, during meetings with team members, of everything that is happening and the multiple sources of information received: (1) what each person is saying, (2) the person's inner conversation, and (3) what the context is conveying.

Eckhart Tolle emphasizes the importance of the concept of mindfulness—"totally focused mind" or "pure presence"—and explains the significance of letting go of thoughts that hinder being present in various situations.

Doug Silsbee explains, "Mindfulness is a state of presence in which we are aware of our feelings and thoughts and the habits of our mind, and we can let go of those that do not help us, so they do not limit us." Cultivating mindfulness is a lifelong process that requires detachment from habitual ways of interpreting the world and understanding relationships.

Chade-Meng Tan teaches that mindfulness leads to developing a mind capable of maintaining calm and clarity through training two faculties: attention and meta-attention (the ability to pay attention to our own attention). He suggests recognizing distractions without self-criticism and letting them go as they appear.

Leaders are curious and genuinely interested in understanding their team members. They inquire why people behave as they do, what makes them successful, and what limits them from unleashing their full potential.

In their work, present leaders are aware that blind spots often exist, both for themselves and their team members. They actively work to identify these blind spots and prevent them from hindering goal achievement.

LISTENING
HOW OUR FILTERS IMPACT
WHAT WE HEAR

When you talk, you are only repeating what you
already know. But when you listen, you may learn
something new.

—DALAI LAMA

In an era of nonstop noise and distraction, true listening is a
crucial skill for any leader—and you may not be surprised to
learn it's a coaching competency as well.

The ICF further specifies that coaches have to listen "actively."[1]
Active listening involves paying attention with genuine interest,
to not just spoken words but also body language, beliefs, values,
concerns, and emotions, especially insecurities and fears. This
type of listening requires using not only the ears but also the

rest of the body. Both one's own and others' bodily reactions are essential sources of information.

We certainly need a new level of listening due to the higher levels of uncertainty, fear, and isolation and in the face of many contemporary crises. Leaders not only need to keep team members informed and articulate the organization's and leaders' vision, goals, and strategies but also need to listen attentively to colleagues' needs, support them as much as possible, and integrate their needs with those of the team and the organization.

Indeed, your success as a leader hinges much more on your ability to "listen up" rather than talk down. Do you hear only what you want to hear, or do you welcome unexpected feedback?

To actively listen, you have to be present, as we learned in the previous chapter. In the training sessions I offer for professional coaches and leaders seeking to develop coaching skills, I explain the intimate relationship between listening and being present.

MULTITASKING VERSUS THE COACHING MINDSET

Many leaders consider multitasking a valuable skill, but when we are dividing our attention, we don't do anything at 100 percent capacity.

People often start conversations in the office with colleagues who don't stop whatever they are doing. That is okay for casual conversations, such as at the coffee station. But this level of inattention is not okay if colleagues are sharing information that is important to them personally or requires some decision-making.

When we don't stop what we are doing to listen, we are not able to fully engage. We will miss body language and eye contact, and the connection with others will not be at its fullest potential. This is especially important as we engage more in remote discussions online and even more so with international colleagues of different cultures.

We cannot listen and show understanding while thinking about something else or engaging in other activities. In essence, presence and multitasking are generally incompatible. To listen to others, we also need to quiet our inner voice and momentarily stop listening to ourselves so we can listen to the other person. This requires being intentional and aware, especially when that inner voice is very loud.

I often convey this concept using a metaphor that I find very apt: the radio. Our inner voice is like a radio that plays incessantly and needs to be silenced for us to hear others. Even if we can't completely silence it, we can work on lowering its volume.

Listening is not the same as waiting for our turn to speak. A characteristic of leaders that demonstrate effective coaching skills is the ability to listen without the need to interrupt to share their thinking. People who listen with genuine interest focus on the message they are receiving, don't interrupt, and aren't concerned about forgetting what they want to say. As a result, they feel comfortable waiting for colleagues to share their thoughts without the need to interrupt.

Francesco Bassoli, vice president of global procurement at Alcoa, told me,

> I ask my team members to speak, and I listen. I learn from people I don't agree with. I seek diversity in my teams, including individuals without acquisition training, to challenge us, to help us explore something we might not be seeing. One thing I consider is that the majority opinion

doesn't always lead to the best outcome. In my leadership style, it's important to monitor the content of each conversation from various perspectives. I strive to monitor the quality and diversity of conversations. If you seek success, you have to listen to everyone.

HEARING VERSUS LISTENING

Leaders who adopt the coaching style are not satisfied with hearing; they listen. Hearing and listening are different phenomena. Hearing is linked to the physiological aspect of the auditory sense. Sometimes, we can hear without truly listening or giving meaning to what is being heard. To achieve the latter, attention must be paid not only to what is said but also to how it is said and in what context.

Rafael Echeverría, a Chilean philosopher and ontological coach, in his book *Language Acts* (volume I, *Listening*), explains that listening is perceiving and interpreting.[2] It means perceiving with all the senses and giving meaning to what we hear because of understanding not only the words expressed but also the context.

Interpretation is not fact-finding. Every interpretation we make when we listen is made based on our personal filters, such as our history, prejudices, assumptions, values, and preconceptions.

Echeverría explains that problems arise when we give interpretations the value of absolute truths because this leads to discussions seeking to prove who is right. Sometimes, we are more concerned with being right than understanding others' viewpoints. To the extent possible, we must be aware of all the factors that subjectivize interpretation since this leads to a better understanding.

When leaders act with a coaching mindset, they must pay special attention to their interpretations and judgments as well as the meaning they ascribe to colleagues' behaviors or what they have said or done. By committing to fully listening to others, we can develop awareness of our own bias and filters and be curious about our assumptions.

How can we bridge the gap between what we hear (and perhaps assume) and what is really said and meant by another? Echeverría provides three useful steps:

- *Verify our listening*—Paraphrase what the other person said or summarize what was understood.
- *Share our concerns*—Notice not just what the other person said but also what is behind the words. When leaders adopt the coaching style, they try to unveil issues where their team members are stuck.
- *Inquire to refine, correct, and understand*—Listening is opening up to others. The essence of listening is openness. Without mutual openness, genuine human relationships cannot exist. However, openness is never complete. Inquiring allows us to understand the beliefs of the speaker and ensure that we are interpreting what they are saying in the expected way.

When we listen to our team members, we are demonstrating that we value them. When people don't feel heard, they do not feel valued either. This is where active listening becomes particularly important for leaders with a coaching mindset.

I had a client who was very good at listening. He intentionally paid attention to his direct reports and consistently invited them to bring up their ideas for improvement and innovation. Once, a peer told him he was wasting so much of his time listening to their employees. He brought this to our coaching session to explore how much listening was appropriate. There is no formula, but listening is an investment to enhance relationships and demonstrates interest for understanding the unique needs and perspectives of team members. The information gained may allow leaders to make better decisions.

When actively listening, pay attention to the filters that activate within us. When we interact with colleagues, those preconceived ideas can get in our way to openly hearing and understanding what is being said.

Be aware that the meaning we give words is linked to our history. That history can confuse the meanings that others attribute to the same concept. They may well be different. For this reason, the only way to understand the meaning the speaker gives to a concept is to ask, for example, "When you say that doing this is difficult, what makes you think it's difficult? What does 'difficult' mean to you?" If someone says, "I want to be more organized in my work," a leader who actively listens could ask, "What does 'organize' mean to you? What do you mean when you say 'organized'?"

In workshops on communication skills for leaders that I facilitate, I present an exercise: a word is said, and participants are asked to visualize it and later write a description of their mental image. For instance, if I say "house," each person envisions a different house based on their experiences. Some visualize their parents' house, others the house they live in, and still others the house they would like to live in.

When participants share what they visualize, they realize how different images are formed in language, which can evoke different emotional reactions. Understanding this phenomenon creates greater curiosity to comprehend others' worldviews and not assume that people attribute the same meanings.

Being aware of one's filters enables better listening and more effective leadership. And we can be intentional with what filters we are using. We can focus on strengths and virtues rather than weaknesses. Positive psychology focuses on people's strengths and abilities, aiming to identify and work on them. This is a good framework to use to listen to colleagues.

Bill Thompson, executive director at Young Storytellers, says, "I believe that the best ideas come from others, not from me, and that's why I place high value on the act of listening. Listening and respecting diversity, including the opinions of experts and nonexperts, allow us to develop strategies focused on the community's benefit. We appreciate having board members from all sectors of the community we serve."[3]

LINEAR AND NONLINEAR LISTENING

A leader who coaches engages in both linear and nonlinear listening. Linear listening focuses on the last thing the speaker said. For example, if a team member says, "These changes don't seem appropriate to me," the leader listens to what was said and asks, "What makes these changes not seem appropriate to you?" The dialogue follows the sequence of what was most recently heard.

Nonlinear listening, on the other hand, is not sequential. It not only focuses on the last thing heard but also on how it relates to something said earlier in the conversation or in past conversations. It involves paying attention to the broader context.

In the previous example, when the team member says, "These changes don't seem appropriate to me," a leader actively engaging in nonlinear listening might ask, "Last week, you made a similar comment. What makes these changes not seem appropriate to you?" This type of dialogue considers not only the most recent statement but also seeks to connect it with previous discussions.

When leaders take on the task of actively listening, they should let their curiosity arise to explore what lies behind their team members' comments. For instance, if an employee expresses dissatisfaction with some organizational changes, active listening can be the most suitable tool to discover what is behind the resistance to change. It might reveal fear of the unknown or another limiting belief. Perhaps a successful team member believes that certain operational changes could hinder achieving the results they have been obtaining.

If leaders remain solely at the surface level of what their team members express, they may miss opportunities to inquire about the limiting beliefs someone holds or the fears underlying their presentations or statements.

SIX WAYS TO PRACTICE ACTIVE LISTENING

To follow the ICF competency framework and adopt the active listening competency to the work of the coaching leaders, apply these six behaviors that demonstrate active listening:

- Consider each employee's context, identity, environment, experiences, cultivated values, and beliefs to optimally understand what they are communicating.
- Summarize what the employee communicates to ensure a clear understanding of their message.

- Recognize messages that may lead to questions that help delve deeper into the discussed topic.
- Grasp the emotions the employee is expressing through both verbal and nonverbal cues to explore them together.
- Integrate the words, tone of voice, and body language of each employee to determine the complete meaning of what they are communicating.
- Note trends in behaviors and emotions of each employee during conversations to identify patterns of thinking.

Fernando Perla, technology manager at Banco Santander, shares the importance of active listening:

> I prioritize conversations, focusing on results while always placing people at the center of interest and listening. I aim to be agile and take advantage of one-on-one coaching opportunities if a team member requests it or if there are aspects that need improvement. With this, I aim to identify strengths, provide support, and address areas with potential for improvement. Having team members observe, understand, accept, integrate, and nurture their strengths helps them stand on those strengths to tackle improvements, strengthen self-esteem, and enhance their ability to achieve challenging goals, training their assertiveness.

LIMITING BELIEFS

One of the main objectives of active listening is detecting a colleague's self-limiting beliefs. When appropriate, leaders can challenge these statements, always doing so with respect. For example, when hearing that a team member believes they have no chance of success in a particular area of their work, it can be useful to explore the source of this limiting belief. It's surprising how often people believe they cannot do something they have never tried for lack of self-confidence.

In some instances, it can also be valuable to explore the hidden benefits of these limiting thoughts. Limiting beliefs can be obstacles to designing and achieving goals. For example, team members might believe they lack sufficient skills, discipline, or even that they don't deserve to achieve them. Coaching-minded leaders listen attentively to identify these limiting beliefs and challenge their team members to explore and transform them when possible.

A PERSONAL STORY

Many years ago, when I started working for Personnel Decision International, my boss asked me to facilitate a leadership program that I was not very familiar with. The company had a process to train the facilitators that included participating in the audience and cofacilitating before going solo. In this case, my boss requested that I facilitate the training, but there was not enough time for me to get the appropriate training. I just had to go and do it. I was hesitant. I was new and didn't want to say no, but I did not want to fail either.

My boss listened to me and explored what my fears were. She asked, "What is the worst that can happen?" My first reaction was that I'd do a bad job and anger a client, but she kept exploring. She asked again, "And what else is the worst that can happen?" I shared that I was new, I wanted to do a good job, and I was not familiar with the program. She listened, showed understanding, and provided support. Her trust in my abilities and her listening to my concerns allowed me to move forward, do the training, and be successful.

MOVING ON

You've already learned that nothing stays the same. Society changes, as do some situations at our workplaces—now more than ever.

We all need to master the art of asking questions to learn deeply about our colleagues. The first layer tells us little but will give us good hints. We can use our intuition, presence, curiosity, and listening skills—as well as our coaching mindset—to learn what's really going on, finding the hidden factors before they come to the surface. That's where continuous learning comes in, to find out what needs coaching.

CHAPTER SUMMARY

One of the most crucial skills for coaching-minded leaders is actively listening to their team members, focusing not only on what is said but also on body language, beliefs, values, and biases.

Active listening involves using eyes and the entire body, recognizing that nonverbal reactions are a significant source of information.

Current times require a new quality of listening, not just keeping employees informed but also attentively understanding their needs.

Active listening requires being present, as multitasking and presence are generally incompatible.

Leaders need to silence their internal voice to actively listen and understand others.

Genuine interest in the speaker's message distinguishes active listening from waiting for one's turn to speak.

Listening and hearing are distinct phenomena; listening involves perceiving and interpreting with all senses.

Leaders need to be cautious when sharing interpretations, presenting them more as hypotheses than absolute truths.

Listening gives meaning to speech and directs the communication process; it is not a passive activity.

Tools for bridging the gap between what is said and what is heard include verification, sharing concerns, and inquiring to refine, correct, and complete our understanding.

Awareness of personal filters enhances effective listening and leadership, aligning with the positive psychology focus on strengths.

Linear listening focuses on the latest statement; nonlinear listening connects current and past statements for mutual benefit.

Superficial listening may miss opportunities to explore limiting beliefs or underlying fears of team members.

Six suggestions for active listening following the ICF framework are to consider context, reflect on the message, recognize messages that lead to deeper discussion, capture emotions, integrate verbal and nonverbal cues, and notice patterns in behaviors and emotions.

Active listening aims to detect limiting beliefs, and leaders may challenge these beliefs respectfully while exploring their hidden benefits.

CONTINUOUS LEARNING
HOW TO EVOKE NEW AWARENESS

The possibility of innovating is always there if one is willing to reflect, let go of the certainty of where they stand, and ask themselves if they want to be where they are.

—HUMBERTO MATURANA

As a coaching leader, you can improve your colleagues' and direct reports' awareness of the bigger picture by inviting them to see reality from new perspectives. They may even surprise you by uncovering new paths and solutions that were not available—or even visible—before.

You'll also demonstrate to your colleagues that you are open to new viewpoints yourself. Colleagues who see you are not threatened by new perspectives will be encouraged to follow suit.

In the language of coaching competencies, we refer to this skill as *evoking awareness*.

Coaches discuss "changing the observer" in the context of their client work. This refers to the habitual interpretations of reality we harbor through filters and blocks developed over our lives, often unconsciously. You could also call this being stuck in the past. These habits block new learnings.

As explained in the previous chapter, these filters include beliefs, judgments, and interpretations we make and believe. When leaders use the "changing the observer" frame, they model and encourage colleagues to notice the types of observers they are, leading them to become aware that their beliefs and judgments may not always be sufficiently grounded or suitable in all situations, especially new ones that just pop up unannounced.

Interestingly, the discipline of Zen Buddhism encourages adherents to change their context in small ways—such as using the opposite hand to eat—as a way to unlock their mind from established patterns of perceptions.

Being open to continual learning means finding challenging situations as learning opportunities. It includes awareness that as human beings we have blind spots and may be missing the whole picture if we are not willing to look at a situation from different angles and, when appropriate, get help to do so.

GET ON THE HELICOPTER

An exercise I do with my clients consists of separating ourselves from the situation and observing it at a distance from the perspective of a drone or a fly on the wall. When we look at the situation from a distance, what do we see? This opportunity to dissociate or separate ourselves from the situation is helpful to see patterns we could not otherwise see. By looking from a different perspective, we can develop new awareness and grab another piece of the puzzle.

This practice invites team members to be different observers, appreciating the situation from a distance—dissociating—from the perspective of a drone, a helicopter, or a fly on the wall. Another option is to encourage them to view a situation from the standpoint of other individuals connected to the company's activities, such as colleagues in other departments, suppliers, customers, or government institutions—the so-called stakeholders. You could even treat it as a role-playing activity.

Coaching-minded leaders understand that a significant part of their role is to inspire direct reports and other colleagues to continue learning and growing personally and professionally. Therefore, they promote letting go of entrenched beliefs about what is possible and remaining open to new ways to look at the world.

Heraclitus, the advocate of change in ancient Greece, who proclaimed that everything is in flux and thus it's impossible to step into the same river twice, also noted, "If you do not expect the unexpected, you will not find it."[1]

For example, older generations may feel threatened by applying technology at work. From using new software to virtual technology or AI, supportive leaders with a coaching mindset validate their fears and invite them to take risks and try new ways of working, such as integrating the technology into their work. It may be intimidating at the beginning but with practice many people learn and get comfortable with integrating new ways of working that once seemed foreign.

My parents, who are in their eighties and still working as professional coaches, don't let technology intimidate them. They may find themselves challenged, but they don't give up. They ask for help when they struggle and are able to use their computers to communicate with colleagues from all over the world. My mother also became very effective at social media. Many older workers remain productive. They also enrich the workplace with their wisdom.

Various tools exist that help create awareness, including powerful questioning, maintaining silence, and using metaphors and analogies, which I will delve into in this chapter.

Bill Thompson, CEO at Young Storytellers, told me, "I aim to help my team members discover answers, to discover something about themselves. In coaching sessions, I don't have an agenda. I want to assist my people in seeing new possibilities for themselves and their work. I am present, listening, asking questions, trying not to direct them."

POWERFUL QUESTIONING

One skill that sets apart the most effective leaders is the ability to make their colleagues think through questions—about how to solve problems they face and the viewpoints they are using to interpret the situation or concerns that arise in certain scenarios.

Powerful questioning is also useful for understanding and exploring the values that underpin each person's actions. Do you frequently ask how your colleagues go about tackling a new problem or creating new goals? This involves determining what the person believes is important, both personally and professionally, their needs, dreams, how they envision their future, and their beliefs about what is and isn't possible. Your goal is to ask them to step outside their framework of thinking at that moment.

A perfect example of a leader who uses a coaching mindset and bold questions is Reed Hastings at Netflix.[2] As described in his book *The No Rules Rule*, his emphasis on staff autonomy, trust, and active questioning helped his team navigate Netflix's shift from the old business of mailers to the disruptive business of streaming. Today, we take the streaming model for granted, but it was only by the dint of Hastings's questions about transformation that he led his team to discover a completely new type of business.

Old habits die hard. For many leaders, giving instructions and sharing experiences is much easier than asking questions that challenge others to think beyond their current thoughts. The ability to ask powerful questions develops with experience. The art of asking questions requires first being aware of their value in everyday conversations and then honing the skill of asking questions that challenge others or foster insight.

A useful analogy for powerful questioning is that of the iceberg. The coaching leader can ask, "What is beneath the iceberg's waterline? What lies underneath? What is beneath or behind the concerns that my team members bring?" In the last chapter, we discussed the importance of listening and asking questions that require curiosity for what lies under what we are listening to. Above the surface, the leader may get the response, for example, "My colleague is undermining a new initiative."

The team member's below-the-surface thought might be "My colleague fears the unknown and is worried about producing results."

Coaching leaders understand that the behaviors of their colleagues are like an iceberg. By examining the underlying aspects, submerged beliefs and fears generating visible attitudes and behaviors can be identified—a crucial step in understanding. Leaders displaying genuine curiosity delve into what is not seen because it is not on the surface yet can give rise to attitudes of resistance to new ideas or proposals.

EXPLORING FEARS AND ANXIETIES

The ability to formulate powerful questions is an art and requires leaders to listen deeply to their colleagues before inquiring about what they are saying. For example, if a team member feels insecure about a project, the coaching-minded leader can ask, "What is the worst that could happen?"

After these follow-up questions, the direct report often realizes that the worst-case scenario is not as catastrophic as feared, and their fears are not reasonably grounded. But at least they broached the subject and might even plan ahead.

Another useful resource for coaching-minded leaders is to remind a colleague of their strengths and the past situations in which they were effective in handling a challenge. Asking about these instances where challenges were successfully overcome helps create awareness that the necessary capacity to deal with a similar situation has already been demonstrated.

At times, colleagues, especially if they are successful, may hesitate in the face of changes to working conditions, methodologies, or processes because they are uncertain about whether they will be as effective in the new situation. If the leader can capture this underlying fear, they can be much more effective in reducing resistance to change, which is often related to the fear of failure.

Here are some questions that may be useful in these cases:

- What are your thoughts on the new processes?
- What are your concerns?
- What do you think you might need to continue being successful?

EXPLORING THE FUTURE

One of the hallmarks of coaching-minded leaders is their commitment to the future and well-being of their colleagues. When colleagues feel that their values align with their leader's and the organization's culture, it is a powerful force for engagement. Leaders need to identify the personal and professional goals of all their direct reports and colleagues to help them find ways to align projects and tasks with what is important to each one.

Here are some questions that can be used:

- What are your professional goals for the next five years?
- What would you like to achieve?
- What support do you need?
- What is important to you?

KEYS TO POWERFUL QUESTIONING

Genuine curiosity is key to exploring what is really happening to a team member. In this way, coaching-minded leaders step away from the role of an expert at the moment of providing coaching. It may be necessary to show wisdom, experience, and ability for execution on many occasions, and indeed, it is a fundamental part of managerial work. But leaders need to identify the moments when it is beneficial to encourage direct reports to reflect on the challenges presented by their tasks and find their own answers. A leader with a coaching mindset has the intuition to spot the essential differences.

Note that coaching is not linked to prior knowledge about a specific subject or being an expert but with exploring and learning together with colleagues to see what is possible beyond the limits imposed by locked-in beliefs and perspectives. In some ways, it resembles the work of a detective. In the coaching process, the coach and coachee are fellow travelers. At that moment, they are cocreating, generating new possibilities of action together.

While it is true that leaders, to reach their position, gained training, knowledge, and skills that some of their direct reports and colleagues may not have, leaders need to differentiate when it is more useful to give directives versus when to provide coaching. With this differentiation established, leaders can consider such moments as growth opportunities when, instead of sharing an interpretation or a judgment, a question could be formulated.

The temptation to convey personal opinions is always significant, especially in leaders who accumulate experience in specific areas and have not consistently adopted a coaching mindset.

If direct reports or colleagues find it challenging to answer a question, rephrase it. Additionally, leaders with a coaching mindset give their people time to reflect before answering.

THE DIFFERENCE BETWEEN
WHAT AND WHO

According to the ICF's coaching competency framework, the *what* is the issue, concern, or challenge that the person wants to work on.[3] For example, someone might say, "What I want is to be more effective in managing my time. I am very disorganized, and I want you to help me better manage my calendar and activities." In our adaptation to the world of organizations, this is what the colleague wants to accomplish.

However, when leaders applying coaching competencies ask powerful questions, they explore not only what the collaborator wants to do or achieve but also the relationship between that person and the concern. The *who* is the identity of the team member and how they are feeling, thinking, and experiencing the issue. In the above example, the leader needs to delve into what is happening to the team member that they cannot be organized, how this relates to the issue that bothers them, and what inner obstacles they face that prevent them from being as organized as they would like.

In essence, leaders explore who the team members are being at that moment and why they don't allow themselves to be otherwise. They want to know what personal experiences prevent them from achieving the desired effectiveness in a specific area or other aspects of their life. My colleague Marcia Reynolds describes this as "coaching the person, not the problem!"[4]

ONE CLIENT'S TIME MANAGEMENT PROBLEM

I once worked with a client who wanted to be more effective at time management. I discovered the challenge was not the amount of work in front of him but his difficulties in making decisions on priorities due to lack of clarity of the company's priorities. The real issue was not managing his time or the overwhelming amount of work. By exploring his concerns, personal challenges, and lack of confidence, the leader realized what he really needed was clear directions from the president of the company about the strategic priorities and to use them as a blueprint to make decisions.

In this way, the exploration becomes much more impactful and transformative than if I focused only on the what, on how to be more effective in calendar organization. That would involve just brainstorming and identifying steps to follow instead of exploring what makes him disorganized and what unique obstacles he faces in this regard.

When leaders with a coaching mindset are interested in who their colleagues are—what makes them tick or what's really bothering them—they often realize that, in addition to the stated concern, there are underlying situations that, when analyzed, can add value.

THE VALUE OF SECOND-ORDER LEARNING

Chris Argyris was a pioneer in the field of organizational development and focused on adult learning at work.[5] He differentiated what he called first-order learning, where observers do something different to produce new results, from second-order learning, where the change is less in the action than in the learners themselves—that is, in their interpretations of reality. First-order learning corresponds to the traditional problem-solving model. Second-order learning requires openness, courage, and a willingness to challenge one's own beliefs.

In the previous example, perhaps beneath the disorganization, the client might have been experiencing a challenge related to self-esteem and lack of assertiveness. For instance, people who cannot say no, resulting in saying yes to everything, find themselves unable to fulfill all their commitments. Others may fear success or failure. Various factors can define who an individual is in a given situation.

When leaders, using powerful questioning, explore not only the *what* but also the *who*, they delve into more than just the actions. They are examining the person's motivations, fears, and obstacles. Leaders aim to understand what prevents individuals from saying yes or no or what their hesitation is.

Through exploration with coaching-oriented leaders, a colleague or direct report can become aware of what is happening, get new insights, and become a new observer of reality. With practice, leaders realize that sustainable plans result from thorough exploration that fosters a change in the individual as an insightful observer. Such exploration becomes more comprehensive when potential obstacles to implementation are identified.

While this approach may be labor intensive, it proves to be productive. As the old saying goes, "If I had six hours to chop down a tree, I'd spend four sharpening my axe." It emphasizes the importance of preparation and insight before acting.

To ask powerful questions, leaders need to formulate inquiries clearly and concisely and get straight to the point. Questions should be posed one at a time, avoiding a chain of queries that might lead the respondent to choose only the last one. Short, clear, and precise questions increase the likelihood of effective responses.

Alexis Ekizian, head of midmarket sales for Google SpLatam in Buenos Aires, Argentina, shares, "In situations where expected results are not achieved, where some people are not performing, prioritizing assistance for those struggling becomes essential. Identifying the root cause is the first step, whether it's lack of commitment, effort, personal issues, health problems, or emotional challenges. Each case requires a tailored recovery plan."

HOW TO POWERFULLY QUESTION

True leaders with a coaching mindset ask questions focusing more on the future than the past to find solutions rather than to blame. They don't feel uncomfortable taking risks and posing uncomfortable questions.

Creativity is a crucial skill when it comes to asking powerful questions, encouraging team members to think creatively and imagine new ways to face challenges.

Leaders also need to consider these other important aspects when asking powerful questions:

- *Question sequence*—Ideally, ask one question at a time.
- *Tone of voice*—Ask in a friendly rather than critical or annoyed tone.

- *Emphasis*—Emphasize certain points in questions.
- *Language used*—When formulating questions, take the time to choose words that will have the greatest impact on your team member. As Mark Twain once said, "The difference between the right word and the almost right word is like the difference between lightning and a lightning bug."

Here are several types of questions to avoid:

Closed-ended questions—These questions can be answered with a simple yes or no, guiding the colleague to where the leader wants to go and limiting the opportunity for deeper reflection that might lead to transformation. A closed-ended question could look like "Can you really take charge of this? Could you have another option?" To avoid closed-ended questions, modify them by adding "what" or "how." For example, ask, "How would your life change if you take charge of this? What other options do you have?"

Questions including a solution or advice These questions are generally closed and often start with "Shouldn't you," "Could you," "Will you" or "Won't you," or "Did you."

For instance, "Have you talked to your people about this?" implies that, according to the leader, it would be good for the direct report to talk to people about a specific issue. It is also a closed question, where the person can limit the response to a yes or no.

Instead, a better approach would be "In your department, what are the communication channels for resolving a situation like this?" or "What are your options to resolve this issue?"

Rhetorical questions—These may imply a judgment or opinion from the leader. For example, "Are you really going to miss out on that opportunity?" or "Wouldn't you like to get along better with your people?" is limiting. More effective questions could be "You mentioned something related to X. What else do you think could be related to the topic?" or "What would be the advantages and disadvantages of making that decision?"

In these cases, leaders need to be aware of what is happening to them in the situation and review the prejudices they have and then think about what they can do about them.

Questions that are covert interpretations—Leaders should not force their interpretations. For example, asking, "How long have you been bothered by that part of your job?" is presumptuous. Perhaps the person responds, "I'm not bothered by that part of my job." A solution is to use the colleague's own words. "Are you very angry?" can be changed to "How are you feeling?"

Questions starting with "Why"—They can lead to a defensive attitude from the colleague, justifying or resisting the coaching conversation. For example, "Why did you do that?" or "Why did you leave that work pending?" can be transformed into "What factors led you to leave that work pending?" The "why" can refer to past or historical causes that might reveal a linear causality of events.

In addition to avoiding certain types of questions, leaders need to resist making comments while the colleague has not finished speaking. Examples include interrupting or finishing other people's sentences or thoughts. The solution can be simple: count to two before speaking, and if they have finished, also count to two to check that they will not continue. Avoiding interruptions can create opportunities for learning, though of course there are exceptions.

On the other hand, leaders need to be assertive and interrupt when appropriate. This is the opposite of the previous point. Allowing others to elaborate for a long time and go off on tangents instead of helping them focus on the present topic is detrimental to a coaching conversation. An excessive number of details can confuse and complicate the conversation. Leaders need to ensure that the conversation is heading in the right direction and refocus it if necessary. An example of how to do this intervention would be "There was something that caught my attention a while ago, which was . . . Would you mind if we go back to that point?"

Marilee Adams's book *Change Your Questions, Change Your Life* is a valuable resource on the never-ending study of questions and questioning.[6] She posits that our thoughts generally occur as responses to all the questions we ask ourselves. By paying attention to how we think, we will realize that thoughts are responses to internal questions and create possibilities and perspectives in our lives.

Adams distinguishes two types of questions: those of the *learner* and those of the *judge*. Typical judge questions include "What's wrong?" "Whose fault is it?" "How can I prove I'm right?" and "Why is this happening to me?"

These questions are reactive, and it's normal to ask them, but to the extent that we can replace them with learner questions, we will achieve greater effectiveness and well-being in our lives. The learner asks, "What can I do in this situation?" "What can I do to make what I want happen?" "What am I responsible for?" "What do I want to learn?" "What is possible?"

According to Adams, if we acknowledge and let go of the judge, accept it, and replace it with learner questions, we create new possibilities. The concept is quite powerful for coaching work. In the organizational context, when employees consistently receive judge questions, they may be experiencing negativity and frustration. Asking powerful questions can elicit exclamations such as "Ah!" or responses containing phrases such as "What an interesting question," "It had never occurred to me," "I've never been asked that question before," or "From your question, I realized . . ."

THE COMFORT OF SILENCE

When providing coaching, leaders will need to be comfortable with silences as an opportunity for reflection. Silence gives people a pause to reflect and articulate their ideas before expressing them—it does not mean you don't know what to say. When we are comfortable with silence, it becomes our ally, making our conversations more interesting.

Many people feel uncomfortable with silence as they interpret it as an inability to respond rather than a space for reflection. They worry that silence might raise doubts in others about their ability to find words instead of seeing it as an opportunity to reflect on what has just been heard. Silence provides spaces for reflection that allow for awareness creation.

Often, people interrupt and speak out of fear of forgetting what they want to say. This behavior denies the opportunity to listen until the end of the colleague's comments, hindering the ability to ask powerful questions.

When should you interrupt? The best time is when the descriptions received do not contribute to the exploration at hand.

METAPHORS AND STORIES

Metaphors are tools that allow leaders, when providing coaching, to illustrate their points. We use metaphors in language all the time. It can help leaders implementing coaching skills to create awareness of the situation. One metaphor I particularly like is of Zen origin: "There was a toad living at the bottom of a well, and he thought the sky was about the same size as the mouth of the well."[7]

Metaphors are undoubtedly the most graphic way to convey ideas and are easily memorable. In my coaching work, I consistently use them and have found through my experience that, like questions, they are effective when tailored to the situation and the current interlocutor.

Camilo Gómez, the strategic alliances manager for Latin America Google, shares the importance of storytelling as well:

> I seek to communicate stories to my team members that can inspire them. Stories that relate to humanity inspire people. In companies, the importance of stories that transcend and are easy to remember is sometimes forgotten. It's a beautiful way to share concepts and generate behavioral changes in people. I also seek to understand the specific needs of each individual and receive good feedback from my direct

reports. If someone has a conflict and a difficult discussion, I sit down to talk with him about the issue.

FEEDBACK

Another way to create awareness is providing feedback to direct reports. Feedback offers information that allows an understanding of other people's perceptions of their behaviors. It is effective when presented as a dialogue—not as a monologue. It requires specificity. The more specific the message or example shared, the more effective it will be for people to understand the effect their behavior has on others.

When feedback is effective, leaders applying coaching skills helps their direct reports see blind spots, create awareness, and take creative and effective actions that were previously unthinkable but become possible through the cocreation of reality generated in the coaching space. In this space, leaders accompany their direct reports in an exploration that will help them incorporate previously unknown distinctions, thus helping them change into a new, more complete observer who sees things from a different perspective.

Feedback can always be constructive, as its goal is to improve the colleague's performance. It can be encouraging, reinforcing effective behaviors, or corrective, indicating what needs to stop, start, or be done differently.

BEST Model

The ability to give feedback is an art. To be listened to openly and without a defensive attitude requires skills and sensitivities that need to be developed. An effective feedback model is called the BEST Model:

Behaviors—Describe the specific behaviors you observed.

Effect—Explain the effect of the behavior on others.

Stop—Stop and engage in a dialogue, listening to other perspectives.

Take action—Take action as a result of the dialogue.

Examples of the BEST Model

Here are a couple of examples of what that dialogue could look like:

"When you stayed for an extra hour to meet with the client (a behavior), we portrayed a sense of loyalty to the client that strengthens the relationship (an effect). What do you think (a stop)? Thank you for your commitment, and please continue with this level of commitment (an action to take)."

"When you didn't deliver the report on time (a behavior), I couldn't finish my report, and it reflected poorly with the client (an effect). What happened (a stop)? I ask that in the future, if you can't deliver the report on time, let me know so I can share the information with my client (an action to take)."

Leaders who incorporate coaching into their management celebrate the success of each team member and provide reinforcing feedback. They identify opportunities to acknowledge how effort, commitment, and work have produced the desired results. The more specific the encouraging feedback, the more effective it is.

MOVING ON

Leading with a coaching mindset, as you have by now learned, has many elements. With remote or hybrid work, the team has more needs. Trust is more important than ever. And conflict resolution is vital as conflicts can become hidden. It's all about the team the coaching leader builds.

CHAPTER SUMMARY

Leaders with a coaching mindset promote awareness in colleagues, encouraging them to see reality from new perspectives, fostering new possibilities of action to face current and future challenges.

Leaders invite team members to be aware of their roles as observers, recognizing how their beliefs and judgments may lack a solid foundation, enabling them to access new interpretations and understandings.

A crucial aspect of coaching leadership is inspiring continuous personal and professional growth, encouraging individuals to let go of limiting beliefs, staying open to the unknown and uncertain.

Effective leaders possess the skill of making their team think through powerful questions, addressing both problem-solving approaches and the lenses used to interpret situations.

Powerful questioning is useful for exploring individual values, going beyond current thought patterns. The focus is on asking beyond the existing mindset.

Genuine curiosity is essential for investigating and understanding what is happening with a team member.

A coaching leader shifts from the role of an expert or consultant when providing coaching. Coaching is not about prior knowledge but about exploring and learning together beyond limiting beliefs.

If a team member finds it challenging to answer a question, a leader may rephrase it. A coaching leader gives the collaborator time to reflect.

Powerful questioning explores not only what the team member wants to do or achieve but also who the person is and how it relates to the concerns and obstacles they face.

Chris Argyris differentiates first-order learning (doing something differently for new results) from second-order learning (changing the observer's perspective).

Effective questioning requires clear, concise, and direct formulation. Questions are asked one at a time to avoid confusion.

A coaching leader focuses on the future rather than the past and is comfortable with taking risks and asking uncomfortable questions.

Creativity is a key competency in powerful questioning, encouraging team members to think creatively and imagine new ways to face challenges.

Important considerations include the sequence, tone, emphasis, and language used in questions.

Leaders need to avoid formulaic or standard questions, closed questions, questions that imply solutions or advice, rhetorical questions, interruptions, and hesitancy to interrupt.

Marilee Adams differentiates between learner and judger questions, emphasizing the shift from reactive to proactive thinking.

A coaching leader embraces silence as an opportunity for reflection rather than a sign of uncertainty, allowing team members time to articulate their thoughts.

Metaphors and stories are powerful tools for illustrating points and enhancing memorability and are effective when tailored to the situation and audience.

Feedback, presented as a dialogue rather than a monologue, provides valuable information for understanding others' perceptions and encourages self-awareness and creative action.

The BEST Model for effective feedback involves describing behaviors, explaining their effects, stopping for dialogue and listening to other perspectives, and deciding on a plan of action as a result of the dialogue.

TEAM COACHING
THE MULTIPLIER EFFECT

The great achievements of any person generally
depend on many hands, hearts, and minds.

—Walt Disney

In today's dynamic workplaces, teams are vital to the success of
any organization. However, team success isn't just about gathering skilled individuals; it's also about transforming them into a
cohesive, high-achieving unit.

This is where an effective team coach plays a crucial role.
Let's examine what contributes to these coaches' success and how
they lead teams to produce real results, illustrated by a practical
example of their impact.

Coaching teams, as defined by the ICF, is "an experience that
enables a team to work toward sustainable results and continuous
development." It emphasizes that "it is becoming an increasingly

important modality in corporate environments as high team performance requires alignment around goals, innovation, and rapid adaptation to internal and external changes."[1]

Leaders need to develop skills that enable them to effectively coach teams and understand the unique challenges presented for this task. Here is a list of skills leaders need to develop to effectively work with their teams:

- Facilitation skills that effectively engage all participants and keep the team focused to accomplish its goals
- The ability to understand group dynamics and how they affect relationships among members and their outcomes, including discerning the team's developmental stage and facilitating meetings accordingly as well as recognizing subgroups, informal leadership, and the management of differences in perspectives and conflicts
- Listening skills that involve listening not only to what is said but also to what is not said in team sessions—and the changes of energy during the teamwork
- The ability to ask questions to challenge and facilitate the team's learning
- The ability to recognize the different systems the team is part of and how they impact those systems, including identifying all stakeholders influencing the team inside and outside the organization

TEAM DEFINITION

Consultants Jon Katzenbach and Douglas K. Smith define teams as "a small number of people with complementary skills who are committed to a common purpose, with shared goals and methodologies for which they are all mutually accountable."[2]

High-performance teams demonstrate the following elements:

- Optimal number of members
- Complementary skills:
  - Technical
  - Conflict resolution and decision-making
  - Interpersonal
- Commitment to a common purpose, which is the reason for the team's existence
- Commitment to performance goals and what is to be achieved
- Shared focus on how team members will work and collaborate
- Shared responsibility for the results of their work

If you are leading a team or are a member of a team, I invite you to consider how these elements are present or absent. You may spot a correlation between the level of effectiveness and the presence of these elements.

DOES YOUR TEAM HAVE THE RIGHT NUMBER OF PARTICIPANTS?

According to Jill Ratliff, the appropriate number of participants for a simple team is fifteen people, ten for a problem-solving team, and five to eight people for a team that needs to actively collaborate with other teams.[3]

If the team is too large, subgroups can hinder achieving results. Studies on the subject show that teams with many participants can lead to dissatisfaction and lower productivity.

For example, when I was part of the board of directors team of the ICF in 2014, we decided to reduce the number of members from sixteen to nine. The result was highly effective because the smaller number of participants allowed for greater interaction, closeness, collaboration, and faster, more effective decision-making.

IS YOUR TEAM EFFECTIVE AT COLLABORATING?

Researchers Martin Hoegl and Hans Georg Gemuenden explain that quality teamwork comprises six components:[4]

- Communication that is frequent, structured, and open
- Coordination, especially clarity on what all members do and how they contribute
- Balanced contribution from members
- Mutual support
- Consistent and even effort
- Cohesion, including how committed and proud team members are to be part of the team

All teams have multiple relationships within them, and the team coach needs to develop sensitivities to understand how these relationships either facilitate or hinder results. For example, subgroups and specific dynamics related to power and informal leadership often form within teams. A coaching-minded leader can leverage these dynamics for task distribution, choosing, for instance, to give project leadership roles to those who can inspire their colleagues in the pursuit of innovative ideas.

STAGES AND THEORIES
OF TEAM DEVELOPMENT

Leaders with a coaching mindset need to understand that teams go through processes, and there are different needs at each stage.

Researchers have come up with various theories of team development. Some of the most recognized ones are Bruce Tuckman's (forming, storming, norming, performing, and adjourning), Jon Katzenbach and Douglas K. Smith's (performance curve), and Connie Gersick's (punctuated equilibrium).[5]

Patrick Lencioni proposed a model to understand teams that looks at common barriers that teams face:[6]

- *Absence of trust* Teams fail when they lack vulnerability and openness.
- *Fear of conflict*—Productive debate and idea sharing are essential but should be avoided if teams fear conflict.
- *Lack of commitment*—Without buy-in, teams don't engage fully with decisions.
- *Avoidance of accountability*—Teams fail when members do not hold each other accountable for their tasks.
- *Inattention to results*—Focusing on individual success instead of collective outcomes undermines teams.

THE DEVELOPMENT OF TRUST AND PSYCHOLOGICAL SAFETY IN THE TEAM

As we explored in chapter 5, developing a culture of trust is essential for team and organizational performance. And for a team to succeed, trust needs to be present and apparent as it serves as the foundation for effective communication and collaboration. Knowing how to foster accountability while promoting an environment of open dialogue is part of developing trust within the team.

Understanding the influence of open communication and trust is crucial. Without trust among team members, leaders may struggle to cultivate an environment where collaborations and creative solutions thrive.

In this regard, these are some actions that have been proving effective:

Establishing clear goals and expectations—Creating clear goals and expectations for each team member is essential for achieving success. Leaders need to encourage open communication both with and among team members, ensuring that everyone clearly understands their roles and responsibilities. Setting clear goals allows teams to focus on the big picture and maintain a common direction while working on specific objectives. This fosters collaboration, innovation, and creativity based on recognizing individual contributions that support the broader vision of the project.

Setting expectations from the beginning prevents confusion and allows addressing any issues that arise along the way, creating a more productive and positive working environment for everyone involved.

Fostering a feedback culture—Encouraging team members to provide constructive feedback and reinforce positive behaviors is an excellent way to promote healthy communication. It not only facilitates good dialogues among coworkers but also creates an atmosphere of trust and support.

Informing each other about our successes, both small and large, and providing feedback of what is not working are two factors that help team members grow and learn, both individually and collectively. Knowing that we have a safe space to offer both criticism and reinforcement inspires us to collectively overcome barriers to the set objectives.

Leading by example—One of the most important qualities leaders need to develop is the ability to listen to their team members. This will make team members feel heard and respected, allowing leaders to cultivate relationships. Being able to use listening skills to identify and solve problems efficiently shows that leaders care about the success of their team and each of its members.

This attitude of trust and collaboration creates a solid work environment where people are motivated to do their best.

Creating opportunities for team development activities—Social events, workshops, or even retreats are activities that can bring teams together in a meaningful way. These activities encourage collaboration and communication within a team. These experiences can bond coworkers, build trust among them, and give them the chance to get to know each other better while having fun. When leaders invest in team development activities, they can help strengthen relationships among the team members and create an atmosphere of camaraderie and support.

Trust is necessary to create and maintain effective teams. It allows the team to communicate openly and develop a sense of responsibility, leading to success. Coaching-minded leaders need to always be attentive to creating an environment of trust and collaboration.

In the team coaching certifications that I offer, participants and I explore these strategies and various related topics to support leaders in building trust with their teams. For more information, visit my website at goldvargconsulting.com.

HOW NORA REVITALIZED AN UNDERPERFORMING MARKETING TEAM

Nora, a coaching client, joined a midsize entertainment company in Southern California with the challenging task of turning around a struggling marketing team. Despite its talent, the team was plagued by missed targets and low morale, compounded by frequent conflicts and a lack of clear direction. The company was on the cusp of a major product launch, making effective marketing efforts crucial.

Step 1: Building Trust and Encouraging Psychological Safety

Nora's first move was not to push for immediate results but to understand the team dynamics through observation and one-on-one meetings. She discovered that team members were reluctant to speak freely in meetings due to fear of criticism.

To counter this, Nora introduced team-building activities and promoted open communication and intentionally cultivated psychological safety, which is the experience of feeling safe to share personal perspectives without feeling afraid of being judged and rejected. The team-building activities allowed people to get to know each other and understand their current personal and professional challenges, which allowed them to be more empathic with each other. Weekly sessions allowed team members to voice challenges without fear, gradually building trust and encouraging idea sharing.

Step 2: Creating Alignment with a Shared Vision

Next, Nora focused on aligning the team's efforts with the company's broader goals. She identified a lack of clarity in roles as a source of confusion. Through workshops, she helped the team redefine its marketing objectives in relation to the product launch, ensuring everyone understood their contribution to the project's success. This clarity fostered motivation by giving each member a sense of purpose.

Step 3: Navigating Conflict and Enhancing Emotional Intelligence

One significant hurdle was the ongoing conflict between Maria, the content strategist, and Mark, the digital ads specialist. Their differing approaches disrupted the team's workflow. Instead of conventional mediation, Nora applied emotional intelligence techniques, guiding them to express their frustrations constructively. With her support, they learned to appreciate each other's strengths, which eased tensions and boosted team cohesion.

Step 4: Encouraging Accountability and Ownership

To instill accountability, Nora introduced weekly check-ins where team members reported their progress toward marketing goals. Rather than typical performance reviews, these meetings encouraged collaborative problem-solving. This approach fostered a sense of ownership, making everyone feel responsible for the team's overall success.

Step 5: Celebrating Achievements and Fostering Continuous Improvement

With the product launch approaching, the team's efforts started yielding results: campaigns saw increased customer engagement, and key metrics improved. Nora made sure these successes were celebrated, maintaining high motivation levels and reinforcing their progress. Post-launch, she led retrospectives to evaluate successes and areas for improvement, turning experiences into lessons for future projects.

The Impact: Nora's Team Was Reenergized

Thanks to Nora's leadership, the marketing team delivered a successful product launch and exceeded its initial key performance indicators by 20 percent, significantly boosting revenue. The team's morale soared, conflicts diminished, communication improved, and accountability increased. It sustained high performance in subsequent campaigns, benefiting from Nora's lasting influence.

This transformation story can serve as an inspiration for leaders aiming to drive positive change in their organizations. By focusing on trust, vision alignment, conflict resolution, accountability, and learning, real and lasting improvements can be achieved. Nora's leadership shows that a positive impact can be made when leaders prioritize building a healthy team culture.

MOVING ON

So far, we have covered trust, team building, in-the-present listening, and many other aspects of leading with a coaching mindset. But how often in your work experience has your organization been hit with a bolt out of the blue—a crisis or major challenge? Leading with a coaching mindset helps your team and colleagues prepare for future events. If they are not encouraged to routinely consider such events, you're not leading. That's next.

CHAPTER SUMMARY

ICF defines team coaching as "an experience that enables the team to work toward sustainable results and continuous development."

Essential skills of effective team coaching include developing facilitation skills, comprehending group dynamics, paying attention to subgroups and informal leadership, actively listening, asking powerful questions, and recognizing different systems that influence the team.

Katzenbach and Smith define teams as "a small number of people with complementary skills who are committed to a common purpose, with shared goals and methodologies for which they are all mutually accountable."

A group may share common goals but not necessarily the need to collaborate for a joint outcome. A team requires coordination for a collectively accountable result.

Hoegl and Gemuenden outline six components of quality teamwork: communication, coordination, balanced contribution, mutual support, consistent effort, and cohesion.

Tuckman's stages—forming, storming, norming, performing, and adjourning—illustrate the dynamic evolution of teams.

Lencioni suggests teams may face five dysfunctions: absence of trust, fear of conflict, lack of commitment, avoidance of accountability, and inattention to results.

Differences among team members lead to conflicts, requiring a coaching-minded leader to be fair and effective in listening to all perspectives.

Trust is crucial for team success, requiring actions such as setting clear goals, encouraging feedback, leading by example in effective listening and problem-solving, and creating opportunities for team development activities.

COACHING FOR THE FUTURE
THE PRACTICE OF STRATEGIC FORESIGHT

The best way to predict the future is to create it.

—Peter Drucker

The COVID-19 pandemic confronted us with many challenges and found some leaders better prepared than others to deal with them. For some leaders, adapting to remote or virtual workstyles was easy. Others found themselves struggling with technology, resisting it, and experiencing high levels of staff anxiety and frustration.

No one wants to go through such a crisis again. But many scientists are fearful other deadly viruses could spread quickly in our high-travel world.

Just as bad, our world is hardly at peace. Tensions on three continents could erupt and engulf many countries into war, including America. And war is not just about death; it is also about disrupted trade and commerce. We have new forms of warfare as well, such as the disruption of the internet and the electrical grid with cyber attacks.

Are you prepared? Do you have contingency plans?

One specific task of coaching-minded leaders is to invite their teams to brainstorm about the trends they observe in their work as well as the circumstances that are not yet observable.

Have staff members develop a list of the different scenarios that could happen to their departments, products, services, or territories. They need to also identify areas where they could develop emergency and recovery plans should that worst thing happen.

Maybe you think that this doesn't apply to you. Consider how many industries have been hit by substantial changes: book selling, taxis, hotels, downtown service businesses. No industry or organization is immune from change. Remember the BlackBerry?

PREPARING FOR MANY FUTURES: WHAT IF?

We can't finish exploring a coaching mindset for leaders without including strategic thinking. To clarify, we cannot prepare for one future but need to prepare for multiple futures because we cannot predict what will happen.

An essential function of coaching leaders is to identify future trends that will impact the work of their team. As important, leaders with a coaching mindset encourage direct reports and other colleagues to ask, "What if?"

If leaders and their colleagues do not dedicate time and energy to this task, the consequence may be an unpreparedness for the future challenges that lie ahead, resulting in not achieving desired objectives. Additionally, if competitors invest that energy in preparation and are ready, it will be challenging to prevail in the market.

The study of futures, known as foresight, enables the identification of signals that require attention. Ignoring these signals can have negative consequences for businesses. For example, Uber revolutionized the work of taxi drivers, and Airbnb transformed the hotel industry.

Bob Johansen, from the Institute for the Future, suggests that leaders, to be successful in a future of extreme disruption, need to demonstrate a new alphabet in which strength, humility, and the ability to build trust are key.[1] He proposes five key steps:

- *Learn to look back from the future*—Clarity is essential but dangerous. Quick judgment is risky, but not making decisions is even worse.
- *Confront fear*—One way to confront fear is by using video games. Developing skills to play video games is a competence that can be applied to business.
- *Create flat organizations*—Flat organizations don't have hierarchies, and authority is more distributed.
- *Be present even when not physically present*—Employees need to feel their leaders are present even when they are not physically there. Leaders need to be close, even when at a distance.
- *Create and sustain positive energy*—This requires maintaining good physical, mental, and spiritual health.

Diego Quindimil suggests that leadership needs to be agile and flexible in the context of the pandemic or any large disruption.[2] Here are some of the strategies he proposes for leaders:

Share a clear, inspirational, and well-communicated vision— This helps employees understand where they are. Communication is key in times of crisis. Given the uncertainty, leaders need to provide certainties and a map to outline where the organization is heading.

Planning is part of this key strategy. The challenges of the pandemic required leaders to understand employees' fears so they could empathize and provide clear messages that built trust in leadership and the organization. According to Kahil Dirani and colleagues, governments, communities, and organizations were in crisis and sought guidance from their leaders.[3] In this type of moment, leaders need to help people and their systems overcome their limitations and fears that affect performance.

Be willing to embrace transformation, learning, and continuous improvement—Committing to embracing change and modifying the mindset—such as rooted thoughts and beliefs—is crucial. This can be especially challenging for leaders who believe that their success is the result of strategies they intend to just replicate. They must understand that what ensured good results before the pandemic or other crisis may not work in the present, let alone in the future. The necessary change requires courage to step out of the known and take risks.

Demonstrate adaptive leadership—This involves being flexible and daring to delegate, empowering others to seize opportunities and successfully navigate the threats they face.

Adaptive leadership is not just about changing perspectives but also taking new actions that impact employees. This requires openness and valuing others' ideas with the necessary humility. Some leaders find this challenging. In this new era, leaders need to also support others in taking risks and be willing to learn from both personal and others' mistakes.

WHAT IS STRATEGIC THINKING?

As I mentioned earlier, we don't have a crystal ball that allows us to predict what will happen, but what we can do is identify possible scenarios and design initiatives that proactively put us to work for those possible futures.

During my thirty years of work as an executive coach, this theme has always been recurrent. That's why I decided to train in foresight, the study of futures, to better understand how to support my clients so they can prepare and create alternatives to navigate those futures.

To achieve this, I obtained two certifications, one from the Institute for the Future in Palo Alto and another from the department of technology at the University of Houston. These programs allowed me to develop new skills and sensibilities to effectively carry out my coaching work.

Studying futures allows us to prepare to understand and be aware of trends and signals of change. Leaders with a coaching mindset prepare for the future by investing time and resources to be ready for challenges that may arise and to create the desired future. They know that success in the present does not guarantee success in the future, so they pay close attention to signs indicating threats and opportunities. This is equivalent to saying that they need to think strategically.

Strategic thinking is the ability to envision futures. It requires not just investing time in planning and solving present situations but also dedicating energy to identify what needs to be improved and what has to be different if we want to be ready for future challenges.

One specific task of strategic leaders is to invest time in inviting their teams to participate in brainstorming possible trends and problems, specifically areas where they could proactively take action to offset the problem and navigate futures successfully. Brainstorming can also be about positive events that could influence the organization.

An essential mindset here is to realize such brainstorming is part of the job in addition to defining and reaching quarterly and annual goals.

We can incorporate the metaphor of going to the gym to get in shape into our work environment and thus ask ourselves how leaders and organizations can be fit for those futures. This involves developing resilience to have the strength needed to face the challenges we encounter, arousing a new awareness in collaborators, and at the same time, paying special attention to these issues and developing new skills that connect us with possible futures.

Florencia Sabatini, communications director at Google Latin America, highlights the importance of safe spaces to promote strategic thinking:

In today's workplace, stress generates anxiety in both written and verbal interactions, as well as in face-to-face encounters. Anxiety leads to difficulty in decision-making, low performance, fear of making mistakes, constant inquiries, angrily written emails, explosive and inappropriate tones, and disproportionate reactions when emails are not responded to quickly. In response to this, I seek, when I judge it necessary, to talk to people by bypassing hierarchical levels, stepping out of the structure to achieve what is needed. I am attentive to making resources available to employees, taking care of my mental health and theirs through workshops, meditation, and physical exercise. It is essential to create spaces to deal with stress, develop awareness of everyone's health, sleep adequately, and seek support in technology.

DEVELOPING STRATEGIC SKILLS

Global trends require leaders to develop higher levels of patience, resilience, flexibility, emotional intelligence, social intelligence, and cultural intelligence. These sensitivities allow leaders to address issues of diversity, inequality, technology, AI, and systemic thinking.

The changes happening around us present opportunities, though not for everyone. Leaders who benefit from these opportunities are those willing to invest time and energy in being prepared to navigate the challenges posed by this VUCA (volatile, uncertain, complex, and ambiguous) and BANI (brittle, anxious, nonlinear, and incomprehensible) world in which we live, as described in chapter 3 on mindset.

Foresight techniques involve developing specific skills, such as framing, research, forecasting, visioning, planning, and implementation, which require leaders with a coaching mindset to commit to dedicating time and energy to these strategic tasks:

Framing—Define what will be studied, and limit the scope of work.

Research—Collect information from different sources. Identify which voices need to be heard.

Forecasting—Based on research, identify possible scenarios and what different situations may arise.

Visioning—Define what the desired future is and use their imagination to create that future after identifying which elements they want to be present.

Planning—Design the steps to take for the vision to take shape.

Implementation—Move into action, and set the plan in motion.

Future preparedness is a state achieved through the practice of strategic foresight with an awareness of the larger systems an organization is a part of and on which it depends.

Leaders need to adopt frameworks, tools, and practices that allow them to detect changes on the horizon, threats, and opportunities; respond by discovering the implications of change and planning accordingly; and evolve to thrive in the changing environment. They also need to pay attention to signals from the future by scanning the horizon, testing assumptions about what is changing, and broadening perspectives and challenge the status quo.

ARTIFICIAL INTELLIGENCE IN THE WORKPLACE

Strategic leaders embrace AI as part of their work and do not fear it. While this technology will replace the work of many people, it will also create opportunities for new occupations. Leaders recognize its value and integrate it instead of fearing and resisting it. As leaders with a coaching mindset can acknowledge the value of AI and integrate it instead of resisting it, they will find better ways to adapt to the reality we live in.

AI manifests in different ways, depending on the industry and the specifics of the organizations we are part of. For example, ChatGPT chat can provide resources for analyzing information or using platforms to receive coaching services with AI software.

Programs already accessible to the public can offer a simple and basic coaching process. While they do not develop interpersonal relationships, these programs provide tools and resources for personal development work.

My word of advice: prepare. You don't know what the next surprise may be. What's more, something developing right now in plain sight could impact you. Think strategically. And here are some examples to get you thinking.

THE FUTURE OF HUMANOID ROBOTS: OPPORTUNITIES AND CHALLENGES

The humanoid robot industry is set for remarkable growth, with forecasts predicting a market size ranging from $38 billion by 2035, as projected by Goldman Sachs, to an astounding $24 trillion according to Ark Invest.[4] In the United States, Morgan Stanley anticipates that by 2050, 63 million humanoid robots could be in use, impacting 75 percent of occupations and 40 percent of workers.

Job Disruption and Labor Shortages

Humanoid robots are poised to address global labor shortages in such sectors as elderly care, manufacturing, and hazardous work environments. By 2030, the United States is expected to face a 25 percent dependency ratio among people over seventy, which will increase the demand for robotic support in healthcare and social services. This trend is evident as populations age and birth rates decline across Asia and Europe, making robotics essential for these economies.

Prices for humanoid robots are also dropping rapidly, with high-end models decreasing from $250,000 to $150,000 in just a year—a significant 40 percent reduction.

Broad Societal Impact

The widespread adoption of humanoid robots could potentially lower the costs of goods and services while freeing humans to pursue creative and fulfilling endeavors. This shift could redefine the nature of work and transform our societal and economic structures.

In reflecting on these developments, we find ourselves at the cusp of a new era. While challenges exist, they come hand in hand with opportunities for growth and innovation. By understanding the potential and preparing for the inevitable changes, we can shape a future where technology and humanity coexist harmoniously, fostering resilience and prosperity for all. But these new developments will require agile leaders with a coaching mindset capable of enabling their direct reports and colleagues to accept reality and plan appropriately.

Just in case this chapter hasn't fully grabbed your attention, what follows are strong recommendations for your survival and success.

FUTURE-READY LEADERSHIP: THRIVING AMID CONSTANT CHANGE

The world around us is undergoing rapid and profound transformations—technological breakthroughs, unpredictable global events, and shifting cultural norms are reshaping industries at an extraordinary pace. These sweeping changes demand a new breed of leadership, one capable of steering through uncertainty with courage and vision. To not only survive but excel in these volatile and complex times requires what we'll call *future-ready leadership*.

At its core, future-ready leadership is about cultivating the ability to anticipate, adapt, and innovate in response to constant change. It's less focused on managing the present and more about proactively preparing for what lies ahead. This dynamic approach prioritizes resilience, learning, and forward-thinking strategies, empowering leaders to prepare their teams for the challenges and opportunities of tomorrow.

When leaders take steps to be future-ready, they cultivate organizations that are not just reactive but fundamentally proactive—poised to seize emerging opportunities and remain competitive in an evolving landscape.

WHY PREPARING FOR
THE FUTURE MATTERS

The demand for future-focused leadership is driven by global trends that continue to reshape the business environment. Here are a few key forces at play:

Technological transformation—Automation, AI, and digitization are revolutionizing how businesses operate. Leaders need to balance innovation with preparing their teams to thrive in this tech-driven world.

Uncertainty on a global scale—Economic shifts, geopolitical issues, and societal changes make navigating unpredictability a critical skill for leaders.

Changing workforce dynamics—With the rise of remote work, gig employment, and multigenerational teams, traditional approaches to leadership need a fresh, inclusive reboot.

Ethics and responsibility—From climate change to social equity, leaders are pressed to make decisions that align business practices with a greater sense of responsibility toward society and the environment.

Without a strong foundation in future-ready leadership, organizations risk stagnation or irrelevance in a world of constant shifts.

THE CRUCIAL TRAITS OF
FUTURE-READY LEADERS

To effectively lead in an always-changing world, key traits are nonnegotiable. The following qualities help leaders rise to dynamic challenges while setting others up for success.

- *Visionary thinking*—True visionaries don't just stare at immediate targets. They imagine how their organizations can sustain positive growth well into the future. They explore trends, identify opportunities, and build strategies to guide their teams toward them.
- *Agility and adaptability*—The only certainty is change. Future-ready leaders foster flexibility, refusing to fear challenges and instead seizing them as opportunities for growth and reinvention.
- *Digital proficiency*—Digital tools have become an integral part of today's organizations. Leaders need to understand how to leverage these tools, from AI to data analytics, to inform decisions and streamline processes.
- *Empathy and inclusive thinking*—Empathy fosters trust, collaboration, and innovation. Leaders cultivate environments where every team member feels valued, recognizing that diversity and inclusion are essential for creativity and resilience.
- *Resilience in the face of setbacks*—Uncertainty comes with setbacks. Great leaders show emotional strength and guide their teams to rebound from failures stronger than before.

- *Lifelong learning*—With the pace of change accelerating, a commitment to continuous learning keeps leaders adaptable. A growth mindset allows them to meet the demands of the future with confidence.

STEPS FOR BECOMING A FUTURE-READY LEADER

Developing future-ready leadership isn't an overnight transformation. It's a continuous, intentional effort. Here's how to position yourself for what's to come:

- *Commit to continuous education*—Stay curious. Attend leadership workshops, stay informed about global trends, and encourage your team members to grow their skill set. Continuous learning empowers leaders and teams alike.
- *Foster a culture of innovation*—Encourage creativity across your organization. Reward experimentation and innovation to ensure your team is equipped to pivot when new challenges arise.
- *Utilize technology thoughtfully*—Stay ahead of the curve by integrating advanced tools that boost productivity and collaboration. Initiatives such as digitizing workflows or adopting AI can position your organization for smoother transitions into the future.
- *Lead with emotional intelligence*—Great leaders don't just rely on technical skills. They communicate effectively, empathize with their teams, and build trust. Emotional intelligence allows leaders to connect deeply with their employees and build stronger relationships.

- *Engage across generations*—Modern workplaces feature diverse age groups, each offering unique strengths. Future-focused leaders make space for cross-generational collaboration, uniting varying perspectives to drive innovation.
- *Prioritize sustainability*—The next generation of consumers and employees increasingly values organizations that act responsibly. Align your business strategies with environmental and ethical goals to reflect what truly matters.
- *Plan for multiple scenarios*—Thinking ahead means imagining various possible futures. Develop strategies for different scenarios to ensure that your organization is agile and prepared to tackle challenges as they emerge.

LEADING BY EXAMPLE

Future-ready leadership requires bold examples. Consider Sundar Pichai, who has steered Alphabet through disruptions by focusing on responsible AI development. Or Mary Barra, who guided General Motors into the electric vehicle era. These leaders adapted to emerging trends with courage, aligning innovation with integrity.

PREPARING FOR WHAT'S NEXT

The world isn't slowing down, and the pace of change will only accelerate. This makes future-ready leadership a necessary mindset, not a temporary trend. To remain competitive, leaders need to be resilient, innovative, and adaptable, constantly fine-tuning their approach to meet the demands of a shifting landscape.

The question isn't whether challenges will arise but how you'll rise to meet them. Great leadership isn't about perfection: it's about action, empathy, and vision. By positioning yourself as a future-ready leader, you can inspire your teams and guide your organization to thrive, even in the unknown.

The world will continue to evolve. The question is, will you evolve with it?

CHAPTER SUMMARY

A transcendent function of coaching-minded leaders is to identify future trends that will affect the work of their teams. Neglecting this task may result in unpreparedness for future challenges and, consequently, not achieving desired goals.

Foresight, the study of futures, helps identify signals that need attention because ignoring them can have potential negative consequences for businesses.

According to Bob Johansen, leaders need to demonstrate a new alphabet for success in a future of extreme disruption, emphasizing strength, humility, and the ability to build trust. Suggestions include looking retrospectively from the future, addressing fear (using video games), creating flat organizations with distributed authority, being present even when physically absent, and sustaining positive energy.

Strategic thinking involves the capacity to visualize the future, investing time in planning rather than just solving present situations.

A specific task of a strategic leader is to involve teams in brainstorming about trends in their work and identifying areas for proactive action.

Global trends require leaders to develop higher levels of patience, resilience, flexibility, emotional, social, and cultural intelligence to address diversity, inequality, technology, AI, and systemic thinking in the VUCA world.

Foresight techniques require specific skills such as framing, research, forecasting, envisioning, planning, and implementation.

Leaders need to adopt frameworks, tools, and practices to detect changes, respond to implications, and evolve in a changing environment.

Leaders need to pay attention to future signals, including scanning the horizon, testing assumptions, expanding viewpoints, and challenging the status quo.

The integration of AI in leaders' work is crucial. Accepting its value and incorporating it rather than resisting it will lead to better adaptation to the current reality. Likewise, the growing use of robotics needs to be acknowledged, coached, and added to strategic plans.

FINAL REFLECTIONS

The current global landscape encourages the development of organizational cultures that prioritize the well-being and satisfaction of human capital. It motivates employees to be imaginative and engage in cocreating effective tactics and strategies to successfully navigate the present and envision valid resources for each of the possible futures.

I hope that the distinctions and strategies shared in this book assist you in incorporating these coaching skills into your leadership. From my perspective, these skills are essential for achieving extraordinary results alongside your teams.

As I did at the beginning of the book, I invite you to share with me your insights from what you have read and the experiences you have gained from applying the content of these pages within your organization.

NOTES

Chapter 1

1. Quindimil, *Mundo Post COVID*.

2. Clifton and Harter, *It's the Manager*; Gallup, *Global Emotions Report 2019*.

3. Gallup, *State of the Global Workplace 2023*.

4. IFC, "ICF Core Competencies."

5. IFC and PwC, *2020 ICF Global Coaching Study*.

6. Dirani et al., "Leadership Competencies."

7. Wilson, "Three Reasons."

8. Schwantes, "4 Signs to Instantly Identify a Great Leader."

9. Brownlee, "7 Leadership Traits."

10. Globex International, *Globex Update: Health and Benefits*, August 2020, https://globexintl.com/wp-content/uploads/2020/09/HB-August-2020.pdf.

11. ICF and PwC, *2020 ICF Global Coaching Study*.

12. Bennis, *On Becoming a Leader*.

13. Maxwell, *21 Irrefutable Laws*.

14. Stevenson, *Better: The Fundamentals of Leadership*.

15. Rath and Conchie, *Strengths Based Leadership*.

16. Goleman, "Leadership That Gets Results."

17. Parekh, "Leadership Development Trends."

18. Goleman, "Leadership That Gets Results."

19. ICF and PwC, *2020 ICF Global Coaching Study*.

Chapter 2

1. Treviño, Hartman, and Brown, "Moral Person and Moral Manager."

2. Northouse, *Leadership*.

3. ICF, "ICF Core Competencies."

4. Escalante, *Integrity*.

5. Carroll and Shaw, *Ethical Maturity*.

6. Ethics Centre, "What Is Ethics?"

Chapter 3

1. ICF, "ICF Core Competencies."

2. Goldvarg, *Supervisión de Coaching*.

3. Kline, *More Time to Think*.

4. McLean, *Self as Coach, Self as Leader*.

5. Bennis and Nanus, *Leaders*.

6. Cascio, "Facing the Age of Chaos."

Chapter 4

1. Gallup, *Creating an Exceptional Onboarding Journey*.

2. Gallup, *State of the Global Workplace 2024*.

3. Hadley and Wright, "We're Still Lonely at Work."

Chapter 5

1. Covey, *Speed of Trust*.

2. Edelman Trust Institute, *2024 Edelman Trust Barometer*.

3. Rizzolatti and Sinigaglia, "The Mirror Mechanism."

4. Brown, *Dare to Lead*.

5. Brown, *Dare to Lead*.

6. Gallup, *State of the Global Workplace 2023*.

7. Covey, *Speed of Trust*.

Chapter 6

1. ICF, "ICF Core Competencies."

2. Fishman, "The Anarchist's Cookbook."

3. Tolle, *Power of Now*.

4. Silsbee, *Mindful Coach*.

5. Silsbee, *Presence-Based Coaching*.

6. Tan, *Search Inside Yourself*.

Chapter 7

1. ICF, "ICF Core Competencies."

2. Echeverría, *Actos del Lenguaje—Volumen I, La Escucha*.

3. Goldvarg, Mathews, and Perel, *Professional Coaching Competencies*.

Chapter 8

1. Heraclitus's philosophy is primarily known through secondary sources, including works by Plato, Aristotle, and later Stoic philosophers who quoted or paraphrased him.

2. Hastings and Meyer, *No Rules Rule*.

3. ICF, "ICF Core Competencies."

4. Reynolds, *Coach the Person, Not the Problem*.

5. Argyris and Schon, *Organizational Learning*.

6. Adams, *Change Your Questions, Change Your Life*.

7. The story is traditionally linked to "The Toad in the Well," an ancient Chinese parable found in various classical texts. It is most notably mentioned in *Zhuangzi* (*Chuang Tzu*), a foundational Taoist

text attributed to the philosopher Zhuang Zhou (369–286 BCE). This text uses parables and anecdotes to illustrate Taoist philosophy, including themes of perspective, wisdom, and understanding the vastness of the world.

Chapter 9

1. ICF, "ICF Core Competencies."

2. Katzenbach and Smith, *Wisdom of Teams*.

3. Ratliff, *Leadership through Trust*.

4. Hoegl and Gemuenden, "Teamwork Quality."

5. Tuckman, "Developmental Sequence in Small Groups"; Katzenbach and Smith, *Wisdom of Teams*; and Gersick, "Revolutionary Change Theories."

6. Lencioni, *Five Dysfunctions of a Team*.

Chapter 10

1. Johansen, *New Leadership Literacies*.

2. Quindimil, *Mundo Post COVID*.

3. Dirani et al., "Leadership Competencies."

4. Diamandis, *2025-2035 Metatrend Report*.

BIBLIOGRAPHY

Adams, Marilee. *Change Your Questions, Change Your Life*. San Francisco, CA: Berrett-Koehler, 2009.

Argyris, Chris, and Donald Schon. *Organizational Learning: A Theory of Action Perspective*. Reading, MA: Addison-Wesley, 1978.

Bennis, Warren. *On Becoming a Leader*. New York: Basic Books, 1989.

Bennis, Warren, and Burt Nanus. *Leaders: The Strategies for Taking Charge*. New York: Harper & Row, 1985.

Bradberry, Travis, and Jean Greaves. *Emotional Intelligence 2.0*. San Diego, CA: TalentSmart, 2009.

Brown, Brené. *Dare to Lead: Brave Work, Tough Conversations, Whole Hearts*. New York: Random House, 2018.

Brownlee, Dana. "7 Leadership Traits for the Post COVID-19 Workplace." *Forbes*, May 7, 2020. https://www.forbes.com/sites/danabrownlee/2020/05/07/7-leadership-traits-for-the-post-covid-19-workplace/.

Carroll, Michael, and Elisabeth Shaw. *Ethical Maturity in the Helping Professions: Making Difficult Life and Work Decisions*. London: Jessica Kingsley, 2013.

Cascio, Jamais. "Facing the Age of Chaos." *Medium*, April 29, 2020. https://medium.com/@cascio/facing-the-age-of-chaos-b00687b1f51d.

Clifton, Jim, and Jim Harter. *It's the Manager: Moving from Boss to Coach*. Washington, DC: Gallup, 2019.

Clutterbuck, David. *Coaching the Team at Work 2: The Definitive Guide to Team Coaching*. London: Nicholas Brealey, 2020.

Covey, Stephen M. R. *The Speed of Trust: The One Thing That Changes Everything*. New York: Free Press, 2006.

De Hoogh, Annebel H. B., and Deanne N. den Hartog. "Ethical and Despotic Leadership: Relationships with Leaders' Social Responsibility, Top Management Team Effectiveness, and Subordinates' Optimism: A Multi-Method Study." *The Leadership Quarterly* 19, no. 3 (June 2008): 297–311. https://doi.org/10.1016/j.leaqua.2008.03.002.

De Hoogh, Annebel H. B., and Deanne N. den Hartog. "Ethical Leadership: The Socially Responsible Use of Power." In *Power and Interdependence in Organizations*, edited by Dean Tjosvold and Barbara Wisse, 338–354. Cambridge: Cambridge University Press, 2009.

Diamandis, Peter H. *2025-2035 Metatrend Report: The Rise of Humanoid Robots*. Abundance 360, 2024. https://metatrendreport.com/humanoid-robots-c.

DiGirolamo, Joel A., and J. Thomas Tkach. "An Exploration of Managers and Leaders Using Coaching Skills." *Consulting Psychology Journal: Practice and Research* 71, no. 3 (2019): 195–218. https://doi.org/10.1037/cpb0000138.

Dirani, Khalil M., Mehrangiz Abadi, Amin Alizadeh, Bhagyashree Barhate, Rosemary Capuchino Garza, Noeline Gunasekara, Ghassan Ibrahim, and Zachery Majzun. "Leadership Competencies and the Essential Role of Human Resource Development in Times of Crisis: A Response to Covid-19 Pandemic." *Human Resource Development International* 23, no. 4 (2020): 380–394.

Echeverría, Rafael. *Actos del Lenguaje—Volumen I, La Escucha.* Buenos Aires: Ediciones Granica, 2017.

Edelman Trust Institute. *2024 Edelman Trust Barometer: Global Report.* January 2024. https://www.edelman.com/sites/g/files /aatuss191/files/2024-02/2024%20Edelman%20Trust%20Barometer %20Global%20Report_FINAL.pdf.

Escalante, Alejandro. *Integrity: The Language of Possibility.* Málaga: ExLibric, 2020.

Ethics Centre. "What Is Ethics?" April 13, 2020. https://ethics.org.au /knowledge/what-is-ethics/.

Fishman, Charles. "The Anarchist's Cookbook." *Fast Company,* July 1, 2004. https://www.fastcompany.com/50426/anarchists-cookbook.

Gallup. *Creating an Exceptional Onboarding Journey for New Employees.* 2019. https://acrip.co/contenidos-acrip/gallup/2020 /octubre/gallup-perspective-creating-an-exceptional-onboarding -journey-for-new-employees.pdf.

Gallup. *Global Emotions Report 2019.* 2019. https://www.gallup.com /analytics/248906/gallup-global-emotions-report-2019.aspx.

Gallup. *State of the Global Workplace: 2023 Report.* 2023. https:// www.scribd.com/document/651992676/Gallup-State-of-the -Global-Workplace-2023-Report.

Gallup. *State of the Global Workplace: 2024 Report.* 2024. https:// www.scribd.com/document/758783089/state-of-the-global -workplace-2024-report.

Gersick, Connie J. G. "Revolutionary Change Theories: A Multilevel Exploration of the Punctuated Equilibrium Paradigm." *Academy of Management Review* 16, no. 1 (January 1991): 10–36.

Globex International. *Globex Update: Health and Benefits.* August 2020. https://globexintl.com/wp-content/uploads/2020/09/HB -August-2020.pdf.

Goldvarg, Damián. *Supervisión de Coaching.* Buenos Aires: Ediciones Granica, 2017.

Goldvarg, Damián, Patricia Mathews, and Norma Perel. *Professional Coaching Competencies: The Complete Guide.* Arroyo Grande, CA: Executive College Press, 2018.

Goleman, Daniel. "Leadership That Gets Results." *Harvard Business Review* 78, no. 2 (2000): 78–90. https://hbr.org/2000/03 /leadership-that-gets-results.

Hadley, Constance N., and Sarah L. Wright. "We're Still Lonely at Work." *Harvard Business Review*, November–December 2024.

Hastings, Reed, and Erin Meyer. *No Rules Rules: Netflix and the Culture of Reinvention.* New York: Penguin Press, 2020.

Hoegl, Martin, and Hans Georg Gemuenden. "Teamwork Quality and the Success of Innovative Projects: A Theoretical Concept and Empirical Evidence." *Organization Science* 12, no. 4 (August 2002): 1–27.

International Coaching Federation. "ICF Core Competencies." https://coachingfederation.org/credentials-and-standards/core -competencies.

International Coaching Federation. *2019—Building Strong Coaching Cultures for the Future.* International Coaching Federation, 2019. https://coachingfederation.org/research/building-a-coaching-culture.

International Coaching Federation and PricewaterhouseCoopers. *2020 ICF Global Coaching Study: Executive Summary.* International Coaching Federation, 2020. https://coachingfederation.org/app /uploads/2020/09/FINAL_ICF_GCS2020_ExecutiveSummary.pdf.

Johansen, Bob. *The New Leadership Literacies: Thriving in a Future of Extreme Disruption and Distributed Everything*. Oakland, CA: Berrett-Koehler, 2017.

Katzenbach, Jon R., and Douglas K. Smith. *The Wisdom of Teams: Creating the High-Performance Organization*. New York: Harper Business, 1994.

Kline, Nancy. *More Time to Think: A Way of Being in the World*. Dorset: Fisher King, 2010.

Koehn, Nancy. "Real Leaders Are Forged in Crisis." *Harvard Business Review*, April 3, 2020. https://hbr.org/2020/04/real-leaders -are-forged-in-crisis.

Lencioni, Patrick. *The Five Dysfunctions of a Team: A Leadership Fable*. San Francisco, CA: Jossey-Bass, 2002.

Maxwell, John C. *The 21 Irrefutable Laws of Leadership: Follow Them and People Will Follow You*. Nashville: Thomas Nelson, 1998.

McLean, Pamela. *Self as Coach, Self as Leader: Developing the Best in You to Develop the Best in Others*. Hoboken, NJ: John Wiley & Sons, 2019.

Miller, John G. *QBQ! The Question Behind the Question: Practicing Personal Accountability at Work and in Life*. New York: Putnam, 2004.

Northouse, Peter G. *Leadership: Theory and Practice*. 7th ed. Thousand Oaks, CA: Sage Publications, 2016.

Parekh, Milonee. "Leadership Development Trends to Watch in 2024: What's Changing and Why It Matters." Knolskape, 2024. https:// knolskape.com/blog/leadership-development-trends-to-watch-in -2024-whats-changing-and-why-it-matters/.

Quindimil, Diego. *Mundo Post COVID*. Buenos Aires: Granica, 2021.

Ratliff, Jill. *Leadership through Trust and Collaboration: Practical Tools for Today's Results-Driven Leader*. New York: Mount Tabor Media, 2020.

Rath, Tom. *StrengthsFinder 2.0*. New York: Gallup, 2007.

Rath, Tom, and Barry Conchie. *Strengths Based Leadership: Great Leaders, Teams, and Why People Follow*. New York: Gallup, 2008.

Reynolds, Marcia. *Coach the Person, Not the Problem: A Guide to Using Reflective Inquiry*. Oakland, CA: Berrett-Koehler, 2020.

Rizzolatti, Giacomo, and Corrado Sinigaglia. "The Mirror Mechanism: A Basic Principle of Brain Function." *Nature Reviews Neuroscience* 17, no. 12 (2016): 757–765. https://doi.org/10.1038/nrn.2016.135.

Rovira, Álex, and Georges Escribano. *El Beneficio*. Barcelona: Plataforma Editorial, 2019.

Schwantes, Marcel. "4 Signs to Instantly Identify a Great Leader during Crisis." *Inc.*, March 24, 2020. https://www.inc.com/marcel-schwantes/great-leader-time-of-crisis.html.

Sibisi, Sinazo, and Gys Kappers. "Onboarding Can Make or Break a New Hire's Experience." *Harvard Business Review*, April 5, 2022. http://hbr.org/2022/04/onboarding-can-make-or-break-a-new-hires-experience.

Silsbee, Doug. *Presence-Based Coaching: Cultivating Self-Generative Leaders Through Mind, Body, and Heart*. San Francisco, CA: Jossey-Bass, 2008.

Silsbee, Doug. *The Mindful Coach: Seven Roles for Helping People Grow*. San Francisco, CA: Jossey-Bass, 2010.

Stevenson, Tim. *Better: The Fundamentals of Leadership*. Stevenson Leadership Coaching, 2016.

Tan, Chade-Meng. *Search Inside Yourself: The Unexpected Path to Achieving Success, Happiness (and World Peace)*. New York: HarperOne, 2012.

Tolle, Eckhart. *The Power of Now: A Guide to Spiritual Enlightenment*. Novato, CA: New World Library, 1999.

Treviño, Linda K., Laura Pincus Hartman, and Michael Brown. "Moral Person and Moral Manager: How Executives Develop a Reputation for Ethical Leadership." *California Management Review* 42, no. 4 (2000): 128–142. https://doi.org/10.2307/41166084.

Tuckman, Bruce W. "Developmental Sequence in Small Groups." *Psychological Bulletin* 63, no. 6 (1965): 384–399.

Wilson, Suze. "Three Reasons Why Jacinda Ardern's Coronavirus Response Has Been a Masterclass in Crisis Leadership." *ANZSOG*, April 26, 2020. https://anzsog.edu.au/news/three-reasons-why-jacinda-arderns-coronavirus-response-has-been-a-masterclass-in-crisis-leadership.

ACKNOWLEDGMENTS

I would like to acknowledge all the leaders that hired me over the last thirty years to provide them leadership development opportunities, including coaching, training, and team building. I also would like to thank all the leaders who collaborated on this book and shared their experiences, including Alexis Ekizian, Florencia Sabatini, Fernando Perla, María Inés Gómez, Camilo Gómez, Francesco Bassoli, Bill Thompson, Martin Denzel, and the leaders and colleagues who reviewed the manuscripts and provided feedback, including Alicia Agüero, Susie Warman, Aida Frese, Lynn Harrison, Teo Blaquier, Marcela Bayarsky, Lori Chow, Inga Bielinska, Clara Beleiro, Patricia Gutierrez, Lida Citroen, Norma Perel, Mauricio Goldvarg, Tobias Goldvarg, Andrea Chilcote, James Wylde, Cheryl Harris Curtis, and Jeanine Bailey.

I also want to recognize Marcia Reynolds for writing the foreword for this book and her support to publish this book with BK and Roger Peterson, Neal Maillet, Sharon Goldinger, and Silvana Pereira, who collaborated with me in the editing of this book.

Finally, thank you to my partner, Steve Kalous, and to my entire family, friends, colleagues, and clients who accompany me on this journey of constant learning that is life and support me in all my projects, including this book.

INDEX

ABOUT THE AUTHOR

Damián Goldvarg, PhD, MCC, ESIA, is a Certified Master Coach (MCC), Certified Supervisor (ESIA), and a former president of the International Coaching Federation (ICF) for the 2013–2014 term. With over thirty years of experience, he has worked in more than fifty countries as an executive coach and leadership development trainer. In recognition of his global contributions to the coaching profession, he was awarded the ICF Circle of Distinction in 2018. He also received the 2019 EMCC Supervision Award for his significant contributions to the development of supervision worldwide.

Dr. Goldvarg is the author and coauthor of ten coaching books, including: *Steps to Success, Professional Coaching Competencies, Coaching Supervision: Voices from the Americas, Mentor Coaching in Action,* and *Coaching Supervision.* He has trained hundreds of professional coaches, mentor coaches, team coaches, and supervisors worldwide, offering programs in both English and Spanish. His dedication to personal growth is evident in the influence he has had on his family, encouraging them to receive professional coaching training, including his partner, parents, siblings, in-laws, nephew, and six close friends.

He earned his bachelor's degree in psychology from the University of Buenos Aires in 1987; a master's in counseling from the California State University, Northridge, in 1994; and a second master's and a doctorate in organizational psychology from Alliant International University, California, in 1997.

Dr. Goldvarg has worked with multinational companies, governmental and community-based organizations, and universities, including Google, Microsoft, Shell, Hewlett-Packard, Coca-Cola, McDonald's, Walmart, Unilever, John Deere, Nestlé, SAP, Lafarge, Citigroup, Ericsson, Porsche, Daimler, L'Oréal, Merck, Inter-American Development Bank, United Nations High Commissioner for Refugees, Food and Agriculture Organization, World Food Programme, World Health Organization, UNICEF, United Nations Secretariat, UNAIDS, the University of Southern California, the University of California, Los Angeles, the University of Minnesota, and the Los Angeles County Department of Public Health.

Born in Argentina, Dr. Goldvarg has extensive experience working with people from diverse cultures and social backgrounds. Since 1990, he has resided in Los Angeles, California, and offers services in English, Spanish, and Portuguese. His website is goldvargconsulting.com, and he can be reached via email at info@goldvargconsulting.com. His social media information is available at linktr.ee/damiangoldvarg.

Berrett–Koehler
Publishers

Berrett-Koehler is an independent publisher dedicated to an ambitious mission: *Connecting people and ideas to create a world that works for all.*

Our publications span many formats, including print, digital, audio, and video. We also offer online resources, training, and gatherings. And we will continue expanding our products and services to advance our mission.

We believe that the solutions to the world's problems will come from all of us, working at all levels: in our society, in our organizations, and in our own lives. Our publications and resources offer pathways to creating a more just, equitable, and sustainable society. They help people make their organizations more humane, democratic, diverse, and effective (and we don't think there's any contradiction there). And they guide people in creating positive change in their own lives and aligning their personal practices with their aspirations for a better world.

And we strive to practice what we preach through what we call "The BK Way." At the core of this approach is *stewardship,* a deep sense of responsibility to administer the company for the benefit of all of our stakeholder groups, including authors, customers, employees, investors, service providers, sales partners, and the communities and environment around us. Everything we do is built around stewardship and our other core values of *quality, partnership, inclusion,* and *sustainability.*

We are grateful to our readers, authors, and other friends who are supporting our mission. We ask you to share with us examples of how BK publications and resources are making a difference in your lives, organizations, and communities at bkconnection.com/impact.

Dear reader,

Thank you for picking up this book and welcome to the worldwide BK community! You're joining a special group of people who have come together to create positive change in their lives, organizations, and communities.

What's BK all about?

Our mission is to connect people and ideas to create a world that works for all.

Why? Our communities, organizations, and lives get bogged down by old paradigms of self-interest, exclusion, hierarchy, and privilege. But we believe that can change. That's why we seek the leading experts on these challenges—and share their actionable ideas with you.

A welcome gift

To help you get started, we'd like to offer you a **free copy** of one of our bestselling ebooks:

bkconnection.com/welcome

When you claim your **free ebook**, you'll also be subscribed to our blog.

Our freshest insights

Access the best new tools and ideas for leaders at all levels on our blog at ideas.bkconnection.com.

Sincerely,

Your friends at Berrett-Koehler

MIX
Paper | Supporting
responsible forestry
FSC® C005010